The Basic Guide to

Selling
Crafts
on the
Internet

James Dillehay
member advisory board to the
National Craft Association

A Craft Business Book *from*
Warm Snow Publishers
Torreon, New Mexico

More books by this author:
The Basic Guide to Pricing Your Craftwork
The Basic Guide to Selling Arts and Crafts
Directory of Grants for Crafts & How to Write a Winning Proposal
Overcoming the 7 Devils That Ruin Success
Your Guide to Ebook Publishing Success

The Basic Guide to Selling Crafts on the Internet
ISBN: 09629923-3-X
Published by:
Warm Snow Publishers
P.O. Box 75
Torreon, NM 87061
www.craftmarketer.com

Contents

Introduction

Can you make money selling your crafts on the Internet? Many craft artisans are doing so right now and with the tips provided in this guide you can too.

The Internet provides the opportunities to leverage time and technology for promoting your craft like no other marketing venue. You can reach millions of potential customers at a cost of less than $100 a month. If you have the patience and persistence to learn what Internet marketing is about, the rewards can be great.

According to a recent survey which appeared in the January, 2001 issue of *The Crafts Report*, more craft artists make money online than don't. While some reported earning an additional $500 to $5,000 annually from their Web sites, a few said they brought in over $15,000 in a year.

A different survey said that reported gains in yearly sales of crafts due to added income from a Web site are averaging 10% to 20%.

This percentage will increase over time just as total online retail sales for all products have tripled each year for the past couple of years. People shop online because it's easy, convenient and probably safer than handing your credit card to a store clerk you've never met before.

This guide will help you learn how to use the many different kinds of online marketing to increase your craft sales. I will show you how people search the Internet day to day and how you can profit from learning which keywords they search for.

If you have tried marketing your crafts on the Internet before without success, this guide may provide you with new ideas, resources and opportunities. Just because one approach doesn't work, one should not give up. There are many potential avenues for getting traffic and sales from the web.

Do not make the mistake of having a short term focus about marketing online. Although a Web site can be put up in a day or two, it can take several months to get your Web pages to show up in the search engines, receive links from other sites, learn how and when to use email and many of the other tools available.

I have more than ten Websites up, which all combined receive between 500 and 1,000 visitors a day. Even though it took each new Web page I created about two months to start showing up in search queries, I now have a steady, daily flow of potential customers and a growing record of monthly sales. So be patient, it's worth hanging in there for.

In any business, you want a plan. A plan is even more essential for success on the Internet because there are too many distracting influences. You already understand this if you have spent any time online browsing. You know how easy it is to go looking for one thing and end up somewhere else, "miles" from where you started. If you think browsing the Internet is confusing, try marketing online without a plan!

This book was written to answer issues like:
- *Will MY craft sell over the Internet?*
- *What do I do first?*
- *What tools and equipment will I need?*
- *How much is this going to cost me?*
- *How do I acquire Internet marketing skills?*
- *How do I learn how to create a Web Site That Sells?*
- *Where will I find customers who will want to by my products?*
- *How will changes in technology affect my business?*

This book answers all these key questions and teaches you how to plan, test and evaluate the success of your online crafts marketing venture.

You will learn how to promote your site using search engine placement, links, email, online auctions, banner ads, keywords, publicity, offline promotion and much more.

Many, many craft artisans now make direct sales online as well as gather hundreds of leads for new customers, suppliers, wholesale accounts and contacts with international buyers.

To make the most of this material, read the book through several times. Take notes. If you are reading the electronic version, you can click on the hyperlinked text to go directly to the resources mentioned.

Don't be surprised if you feel confused by the concepts and technology of the Internet described. It may take several exposures to the material before you grasp the bigger picture.

I hope to save you time, money and effort by painting a clear image of what you need to do to be successful selling craftwork online.

Keep a notebook handy during the day, because once you start looking at the many ways of online marketing, your mind will begin to come up with your own ideas. The possibilities and avenues of Internet promotion are vast, exciting and ongoing.

Create your own marketing plan or use the example marketing plan included in Chapter 5. Approach the activities recommended step-by-step. Work with each method until you have mastered that process.

Rest assured that you can learn to do everything mentioned in this book. When the terminology seems confusing at first, don't linger on those areas that do not make sense. Start with the simpler tasks first. Then go back and spend some time attempting to learn what you did not understand. Continue going over the material in small doses. Eventually, you will find that your understanding grows with the concepts and you will see how to proceed.

Expenses involved in marketing your crafts on the Internet can be much lower than the costs of traditional marketing. I say "can be" because there are many ways to spend lots of money and get little results. This book points you to free and low cost resources for marketing solutions first whenever possible.

You don't have to have the fanciest site on the Web with huge graphic images and bells and whistles like java scripts and animations. In fact, sites that do best are usually simple, easy to navigate and contain fast loading graphics. Internet surfers are in a hurry. Statistics say that if a page takes longer than six or seven seconds to download, most visitors go elsewhere.

Join Internet discussion groups for craft professionals listed later in the book. Stay abreast of changes in ecommerce by subscribing to several of the free email newsletters on Internet marketing listed in the Appendix.

Once your site is up and running, we'll help you learn how to track your results from all your activities to see which of your promotions are working and which ones need to change or disappear.

There are at least two categories of customers your craft will appeal to on the net. The first is the general public. The second audience is wholesale buyers like stores, galleries and catalogs.

You will find it easier and more cost effective to create separate Web pages or sites for each audience you will attract. Not only will each type of visitor get exactly what he or she is looking for, but when you know who your audience is, you can learn where they hang out on the Net and how to reach them.

A large percentage of people on the Net are looking for free information. All those searches for something free do not exclude or stop visitors from purchasing goods they want to buy. When you take advantage of this by offering free reports or other kinds of incentives, the freebie should lure visitors to another Web page or site where they can purchase the related product.

Your Web site may have several related functions:
• Direct sales of craft products to retail customers
• Wholesale sales to stores and galleries
• Sales of craft supplies, tools and equipment
• Generating leads for your mailing list
• Locating new wholesale accounts
• Supplement your offline marketing promotions
• Expand your sales into other countries
• Create income from affiliate programs
• Host an online catalog or brochure of your products

The appendix is loaded with free resources online to help you create your Web site and get and increase your Web traffic and sales right away.

I will show you many ways to automate routine tasks which helps you reduce the long, uphill learning curve. It would take the average person months to learn about the tips and resources found in these pages.

I use most of the tools I recommend in this book. Before I found these utilities, promoting my Web sites consisted of weeks and weeks of mind-numbing, keypunching struggle, frustration and tedium. Now I can do ten times the amount of work automatically and save my energy for creativity.

Technology changes the way the Internet will affect your business. Sign up to receive a free newsletter on Internet marketing for crafts at **www.craftmarketer.com/newsletter.htm** to get news and updates on techniques for winning at online promotion.

This book can point you toward the door to successful selling online. You still have to take the steps to go through it.

Chapter 1 Why Sell on the Internet?

Should you be selling your craft on the Internet? Yes, but only if you are willing to put in the time it takes to learn online marketing. The mission of this book is to make that process as painless and affordable as possible.

It's a lot less expensive to promote online than many other ways of selling. Marketing on the Internet is easier, too, if you are willing to learn and if you can use a computer.

Don't get me wrong, sales will not come overnight, nor will they come without considerable investment in time, effort and a certain amount of hardware and software.

Of course, no amount of guidance will make a person succeed at Internet marketing unless that person is already determined to be successful. This is no less true on the Net than in other endeavors in life.

How ecommerce is growing

Ecommerce or Internet commerce is growing. The number of online retail consumers has continued to rise even when Dotcom stocks were failing and the economy was technically in a recession.

Artists and craft persons are now selling their work online, expanding their business internationally and increasing their profits every day.

In this guide, you will see quoted statistics from companies like Forrester Research, Jupiter Communications and others. These names are among the most respected research firms supplying Web data. Their marketing reports on trends and sales projections cost thousands of dollars each. We'll show you where to get excerpts from their reports for free.

Who is the average Internet user?

According to recent surveys conducted among 5,000 users, the average Internet user is probably:

• American, around 41 years old, educated and earning good money.

• Roughly 50% or more are female.

• 61% use Netscape Communicator, 56% use Microsoft Internet Explorer,

• 47% are married.

• 75% of searchers surf intending to buy.

• 33% of searchers made a purchase online most of the time.

• Of those who did not buy, over 70% reported the reasons were that sites were confusing and they could not find what they were looking for.

• Of those who made purchases online - up 10% over last year for individuals and up 23% for business purchases - the contributing factors to buying from a site online were:

1) quality of facts

2) reliability

3) ease of ordering

It might help to keep a few things in mind about people surfing the web. They are often impatient, wanting what they want right now. They won't wait for a slow loading site to download.

Like everyone else, Internet users enjoy getting anything for free. Design your site to offer something visitors can take with them at no cost like a newsletter or free report.

Also, Internet browsers like to tell you what they think, much more so than offline prospective customers. This can be good because it opens up the possibility of dialog and later building a relationship with your prospects.

How many people are online?

No one accurately knows how many folks are online because new users sign on daily by the thousands. Several companies, however, have made it their business to gather data on Net usage. Some of these companies sell the information in the form of reports. However, sample excerpts from this material are provided for free.

For purposes of a small business owner, the following sites will give you basic demographic statistics on Internet usage:

ecommerce.vanderbilt.edu/papers.html -- This may be your best starting place for learning what is going on with ecommerce.
www.mids.org
cyberatlas.internet.com
www.gvu.gatech.edu/user_surveys

What the Internet can do for your business

The Internet provides you many opportunities. Among other things, it is an interactive information source, a means of contacting anyone with email anywhere in the world, and hosting a worldwide brochure/catalog for your craft.

For local businesses looking for new customers, the Web provides you a large ad that would be unaffordable in the *Yellow Pages* phone directory. Will local customers look for you online? One study reported that 55% of people use the Internet to find local businesses.

Costs of running a Web site are much lower than selling offline. By reducing your marketing costs, you increase your profit margins.

By using email, online auctions, links, banners, search engines, publicity and newsgroups, you can effectively reach many more people with one message than is economically possible through other traditional means.

By increasing your exposure, you can attract wholesale buyers for your crafts. Several craft persons I have spoken with report increased contacts and sales to stores after they put up a Web site. You may have already experienced a similar phenomena that happens when you have a booth at a craft fair and store owners approach you there.

Why many Internet businesses fail

Save yourself many disappointing moments by reviewing these common mistakes:

1) *Lack of a clear vision and marketing plan* - If you don't know where you are going, how will you get there? This is true in all business ventures, online and off. You can stumble around for awhile trying this or that without any clearly defined goals, but

aimless wandering won't serve you when you face an unexpected challenge.

2) *Lack of the proper tools and equipment* - Internet marketing can be much less costly than traditional marketing, but only when you use tools to help automate many routine tasks. See the next chapter for a list of what you need to make money selling over the Internet and check the Appendix section for more resources. Before I began using these services and programs, I was spending weeks and weeks of long hours trying to design Web pages, analyze my site for higher placement in the engines, construct response forms and design a shopping cart. With these tools, you can have a fully functional site up within a few hours and be promoting it right away.

3) *Hesitancy to buy online* - Reluctance to make purchases online is fading. Statistics show online sales have almost tripled for several years. The concerns and distrust of the online medium is fading. It's probably safer to give your credit card to purchase online than to hand it over to a store clerk you have never seen before. An advertisement appeared in many major publications in May/June of 2000 by Mastercard and Visa assured readers that they would not be held responsible for any unauthorized use of their credit card while making a purchase online.

4) *Relying on myths about Internet success* - You may have heard some of the hyped up stories about people making fortunes online. Unfortunately, a few wild successes make the Internet look like a gold mine for every business. It isn't. Count on putting in many hours in the beginning six months and at least an hour a day for maintenance thereafter. The more time you put into marketing online, the better results you will see.

5) *Poor Web site design* - A poorly designed site is worse than not having one. A good site allows you to lead the visitor through your pages to where you want them to go. For most of us, that means buying a craft product. Statistics show many online transactions never get completed because the customer is confused by the Web site.

6) *Lack of traffic to the Web site* - A common misconception about the Net is that if you put up a Web site, people will come.

People will visit your site only if you drive them there through the various means described in this book. A few of the most essential ways to build traffic include: you must list your site in the search engines, get links from related sites, get publicity in print and traditional media in addition to online publicity, gather contact information from your prospects and follow-up with them via phone or email.

7) Inability to take orders online - The big advantage of having a Web presence is being able to take orders for your crafts online. Without that capacity, many visitors will pass you by. If you don't have a shopping cart built in, at the very least, you will want to include your toll free order number so customers can reach you.

8) Neglecting to collect email addresses of visitors - Getting thousands of visitors is pointless if you can't get back in touch with them. You want a means for people to leave their email or you lose them as prospective customers. There are lots of ways to get that contact information which will be detailed later in the book. Once you have the emails, then you want to follow-up frequently.

9) *Failing to follow-up with customers and visitors* - The secret to getting more sales is keeping in regular communication with your customers, reminding them who you are and why they would want to buy from you. Email is the perfect medium because it costs you virtually nothing to send the same sales announcement to three or 3,000 customers with one click. Two of the best and cheapest programs for managing large lists of email addresses are Pegasus and Eudora Pro. Both of these programs are free. Download the software for PC or Mac at **www.pmail.com** or **www.eudora.com**

10) Failing to stay up-to-date about ecommerce and Web marketing - Technology changes fast. For example, you can't rely on articles written two years ago that tell you buying banner ads are the way to build your business because that information is out of date. Investing your entire budget in banner ads today can cost you plenty and get you little in return. Stay current with what works and what doesn't work. See the appendix for free newsletters to keep you informed.

11) Giving up too soon - You often don't see sales until after six months of promoting through search engines, unless you are linking to your Web site from auctions you set up like those at **eBay.com**. See Chapter 11 on auctions for more details.

Risks of shopping online

Most experts believe that shopping online with a credit card is safer than giving your credit card to a retail store. A large number of credit card fraud cases arise from retail sales employees who handle card numbers.

Internet commerce systems encrypt credit card numbers, thus taking away the temptations of employees who get a customer's card.

For you, ecommerce is not as risky as opening a gallery or store. Stores burn down, get vandalized or robbed.

Your challenge is to get your customers to believe that shopping on your site is safe for them. Following is an example of a customer shopping guarantee we use on our site. Secure server (SSL) is explained to convey confidence. Notice also that not only is the credit card use guaranteed, but the product itself comes with a 90-day money-back guarantee.

Shop Risk Free on our secure server!
Craftmarketer.com's Guarantee protects you when you shop at Craftmarketer.com, so that you never have to worry about your credit card safety.
We guarantee that every transaction you make at Craftmarketer.com will be 100% safe. This means you pay nothing (0) if unauthorized charges are ever made to your card as a result of shopping at Craftmarketer.com.

Why is Craftmarketer.com safe?
Safe Technology: Our secure server software (SSL) uses the industry standard and is among the best software now available for secure commerce transactions. It encrypts all of your personal information, including credit card number, name, and address, so that it cannot be read or viewed as this information travels over the Internet.
Your satisfaction is guaranteed! All of our books come with our 100% money-back guarantee. If you aren't completely satisfied for any reason, return the book(s) within 90 days for a prompt refund! **http://www.craftmarketer.com**

Chapter 2   Tools, Equipment and Skills Needed

Below is a list of tools, services and skills that are basic to building an online business for selling your craft
s. You can, of course, get more elaborate systems and expensive equipment, but you may not want them until your business justifies the expense.

Equipment

One way to save really big dollars was to buy equipment and software that is two or three generations down from top of the line. Once new models have been released - frequently every three to six months - the cost of the next-down versions drops dramatically.

Another challenge to owners of computer and Internet technology is that the rapid growth and development presents more and more options to spend money. Fortunately, the entry of so many suppliers in the field has also created competitive pricing which continues to make purchasing equipment and services a buyer's market.

See Price Watch for comparison of prices and systems: **www.pricewatch.com**

You can also pick up good deals on auctions at Ebay.com: **www.ebay.com**

Computer

Although it is possible to have an Internet presence without owning a computer, the inconvenience of using someone else's system will soon motivate you to get your own.

Personal computers are dropping in price so much, a fast machine with plenty of memory can be owned for less than $700.

Your choices will probably fall into two categories, either a PC or a Macintosh. Mac's are great if you do a lot of graphic work. However, there isn't as much software available that runs on their machines. Go with a PC for getting your business on the net. The chief reason for choosing a PC is that much of the Internet marketing software is not available in Mac format. If you already own a Mac and want help locating software, visit: **www.netprolive.com**.

When shopping for a computer, look for one that is not the fastest computer on the market in terms of megahertz. For example, instead of purchasing a 900 megahertz computer, look for a deal on a system running at 350 megahertz instead. You will save several hundred dollars and probably will not miss the extra milliseconds in speed.

Get lots of RAM or SDRAM. Most newer systems today won't even run with less than 32 MB. If you can afford the upgrade get at least 64MB or 128MB of RAM. The extra memory will speed your efficiency and cut your labor costs.

Modem

You want a modem for connecting to the Internet and for sending or receiving faxes. A modem is a signal modulating and demodulating device that transfers data across phone lines. Many computers come with modem built in or you can purchase an external modem.

The slowest speed modem that will access the Internet efficiently is 28K. Most systems now come with 56K and they are upgradeable to faster speeds via software. Get the highest connect speed modem available.

More options for faster data speed transmission over phone lines are now available in some cities. Two acronyms you will see are ISDN (Integrated Services Digital Network) and DSL (Digital Subscriber Line) connectivity. DSL will speed your connection from 128kbps to 700kbps. ISDN lines boost your speed to 64kbps to 128kbps. In general, ISDN will be a poorer choice than DSL.

You can also go with a satellite DSL or tower broadcast DSL, both at higher speeds than typical modems. You pay extra for these services but if you spend a lot of hours Web marketing, you will accomplish more in less time. Check for availability of these services through your local phone company or by searching the Internet. See DSL Reports at: **www.dslreports.com**.

Printer

You want a printer to print emails, orders, correspondence, flyers, brochures, business cards and miscellaneous reports for your business. Color ink jet printers can be had for around $150 and prices are dropping.

Scanner or digital camera

A flatbed scanner converts photos of your products into digital formats suitable for viewing on Internet Web pages. A good quality color scanner can be had for around $100 at the time of this writing.

The highest quality images will come from scanning slides of your work. Slide scanning devices are more expensive than the flatbed scanners just mentioned. I have heard more webmasters prefer slide scanning for the higher resolution and image qualities.

Digital cameras take photos in digital format that can be imported directly into your image software.

Services and Software . . .

Internet Service Provider (ISP)

If you don't already have it, you will want access to the Internet for research and for uploading and maintaining your Web site. Access is provided by what is called a dial-up account. Providers of dial-up accounts are called ISP's or Internet Service Providers. Typically, when you sign up for a service, you get software that allows you to browse the Internet, an email account, and a newsreader for getting messages from news groups.

If you can afford it, get an extra dial-up account with a different provider. That way, if one of your providers has problems, you can still access the net.

There are many ISPs available both nationally and locally. Local ISPs can be found in the Yellow Pages under the heading "Internet Service Providers." Local and national ISPs like America Online (**AOL**), Compuserve (now owned by AOL) or Earthlink allow you to access the world wide Web through a browser interface, usually for around $20 a month.

For connecting to one of these services, call:

AOL - (800)827-6364

CompuServe - (800)487-9197

Earthlink - (888)earthlink

At least one drawback to these services is that you have to pay to see their advertising every time you log on. You are continually bombarded with promotional messages you don't need or want. Also, when you attempt to dial-in in the evenings - the peak time for Internet use - you often get busy signals. Lack of dependable access can retard your business growth rapidly. In general, use a local ISP for reliable Internet access. Check your *Yellow Pages* for "Internet Service Providers."

However, there are other good reasons to have a second or third account with AOL or CompuServe in addition to your main ISP. AOL has almost 20 million customers, many of whom participate in forums, discussion groups and chats on AOL that are not accessible to nonmembers. These groups are excellent places to mention your product or Web site.

Also, there are many places for posting articles and classified ads only accessible to subscribers. I recommend getting the lowest fee subscription available for AOL and keeping the account for access to their large group of potential customers.

In addition to subscription ISP's, there are a few free ISP's where you don't pay anything for access to the Internet. With free ISP's, you are forced to look at ads which take up a portion of your browser window.

The Free ISP model has not proved successful for several companies who hoped to earn enough revenue from ad sales to cover expenses and still be profitable. Most of the original free ISP's have shut down. Even those left in the field are charging customers for access over 10 hours per month.

You may find the free ISP ads a nuisance to deal with as you will be using your browser window for research which already takes a lot of time without viewing a full screen. Be cautious when examining offers from free ISP's. Some companies have terms in fine print that mean you will get charged later. See **www.freei.net, www.netzero.com,** and **www.juno.com.**

Web site

If you don't have a Web site yet, I suggest you read an excellent guide to building a Web site such as ***Poor Richard's Web Site*** by Peter Kent. This is absolutely the best book I have seen that simplifies the Web building steps. The book contains hundreds of free resources.

You will eventually want at least two Web sites, each with its own domain name, preferably one with your company name and the other with your most important keywords, such as "glass angels" or "gift boxes" or whatever words someone would find you by searching for.

Having two Web sites gets you more pages listed in the search engines. If you can only afford one domain name for now, use a name with keywords that people are most likely to search for you.

Web host

A Web host differs from an ISP in that the host is the address where your Web site will reside. An ISP may provide hosting services. Web hosts will provide a variety of service packages which you should examine closely before signing up.

For one of my sites, I pay $49 a month for a reliable, commercial Web site that provides email accounts, unlimited autoresponders, shopping cart on a secure server. I also use one of the free Web hosts for several of my other sites. The free hosts are clumsy to work with but they are free. Locate them by doing a search for "free web hosting" on any major search engine.

Email

When you sign up with an ISP, you will usually get at least one email account. Email is included in the price you pay for Internet access, usually between $10 and $20 a month.

Email with AOL, Compuserve or a national ISP is fine, but does not allow you to do much more than read and send email. When you begin accumulating customers' emails, you will want the capacity to send single messages to multiple recipients.

For managing large email lists, you want a POP email account. POP stands for Post Office Protocol. With a POP email account, you can do much more than the standard AOL account. For one thing, you can choose between email management programs, some of which provide many functions unavailable through AOL's email.

At my craftmarketer.com site, I have a POP account which allows me to have unlimited email aliases. For instance, someone can send mail to james@craftmarketer.com or info@craftmarketer.com or any other alias I choose. All the mail for each alias will be redirected to whatever email address I choose. This comes in handy when you are running various promotional campaigns and you want to track response rates. You can create a different alias for each offer and then compare results my counting up the responses to each alias.

A POP account is usually standard with most Web hosting services so it is not necessary to enroll for an account by itself. You will also want an email manager to read, send, and manage email. If you will manage large lists of email addresses, use **Pegasus (www.pmail.com)** or **Eudora Pro (www.eudora.com)** mentioned earlier.

There are free email services on the Net which you can get at the following. Juno allows you free email without having an ISP account. The others require access to the Internet to use your email account with them.

www.hotmail.com
www.juno.com
www.yahoo.com
www.bigfoot.com

Internet browser

The two most popular independent Internet browsers are Netscape and Microsoft Internet Explorer. Both are available free of charge from **www.netscape.com** and **www.microsoft.com**.

These browsers themselves are relatively free of advertising, but you will want an ISP (not AOL or Compuserve as they have their own browser built in) to get to the Internet to use their browsing abilities.

As mentioned, I don't recommend trying to run a commercial site strictly from one of the services like AOL or Compuserve. It's good to have an account with them for other reasons described later. For doing business, you want Netscape or Microsoft Explorer because they allow you full access to the Net without all the ads that the commercial services throw at you.

Domain name

An example of a domain name is "yahoo.com." Commercial sites usually choose the ".com" extension, but other extensions are also available like ".net" or ".org". Becoming available as this book is being published are extensions like ".sales" and ".travel".

Domain names convey a solid image that will help your customers overcome any hesitations to order online. Every thing you can do to evoke confidence to your prospects adds up to more sales.

What is the best domain name to use? Most experts agree that your company or product name will serve you better on all fronts. For a business, always register the .com extension first. If you have the funds to invest, also get the .net and .org extensions.

Suppose your company name is more than one word, like Jade's Wood Works. You might register jadeswoodworks.com. You would also want to look at registering jades-wood-work.com, too. The more domain Web sites you have, the more you can make use of search engines to boost your traffic.

Another advantage of having your own domain is that you will be taken more seriously if you use an email address with your domain name extension.

For instance, one of my sites is **www.craftmarketer.com**. Someone sending email to info@craftmarketer.com will realize they are writing to a registered domain name company and a legitimate business.

More good reasons to have your own domain

• Search engines use SPAM filters to identify SPAM originating from free Web pages on other domains. This means that someone else SPAMMING from, say a page on angelfire.com could cause the search engine to disallow other pages residing on angelfire.com.

• Domain names are shorter and easier to remember. For example, spiderweb.com is easier to recall than a name like: www.angelfire.com/ak/webs.asp

• Usually, it is easier to upload and manage page changes to a domain registered site. This is especially true if you use Web page design software such as FrontPage.

• Branding, or name association, is important in any commercial venture even for the artist or craft person. The more often customers hear or see your name, the more likely they will buy from you. Domain names are like brand names. They stick in the mind. So take some time in selecting your domain name.

Many Web hosts offer domain name registration when you sign up for hosting services at no charge or for a small fee.

The original site for searching for existing domain names and registering new names is **www.networksolutions.com**. You can also register at **www.register.com**.

I paid $13.50 per domain name per year through **000Domains.com**, an affiliate of Tucows.com, a very respected Web company.

Another useful reference is **www.e-gineer.com/domainator**. This site checks domain name availability, US trademarks, definitions, synonyms, and similar words.

Run a check for trademarks to see if your prospective domain name is taken before registering your domain because it can create serious problems if you end up with a trademark violation.

The site to conduct a trademark search and register your trademark is **www.uspto.gov/tmdb/index.html**

In general, shorter domain names make it easier for your customers to remember and decrease the likelihood of spelling errors. But you may also consider longer domain names that include important keywords that people will find you. Keywords in the domain name help boost your ranking in the search engines.

Web page editor or layout software

To create Web pages fast and efficiently, select a Web composing software program that automates many routine design and link checking tasks. Here are three popularly reviewed programs and their Web addresses.

Dreamweaver™ - **www.macromedia.com**

Microsoft FrontPage™ - **www.microsoft.com**

HotMetal™ - **www.hotmetalpro.com**

For shareware, freeware or public domain software programs, see the appendix.

Many Web authoring software programs have built-in ability to publish your Web pages to your host. The function of publishing your pages to the Internet is accomplished through what is known as FTP or File Transfer Protocol. In other words, FTP is the technical method by which Web pages get up on the Internet so that others can see these pages.

If your Web composing software doesn't include an FTP function, you will want to acquire a separate software utility for this ability to upload pages. FTP software can publish, delete, and create directories on your Web site with ease. Instructions on how to upload Web pages will come with your software. Some FTP programs are free, some cost. I get good results using WS_FTP LE, available free at **Tucows.com**. By the way, Tucows.com is a great source for free software.

Search engine monitoring software

One of the most profitable tools is the ability to track your Web pages positioning in the search engines for specific keywords that customers use to find you. You want to know if your ranking is improving or declining week to week.

The best program I found for automating construction of Web pages for optimal ranking in the search engines is the previously mentioned, **Web Position Gold**. This software upgrades itself frequently to accommodate changes in the way search engines do their ranking, among many other important tasks. You can download a free trial at **www.craftmarketer.com/web-position-software.htm**.

WordTracker subscription

WordTracker.com shows which keywords people actually use while conducting searches in the search engines. WordTracker offers a free trial, but it's a limited edition of the full scale service.

In addition to listing actual counts of searches done for keywords, WordTracker also tells you how many Web sites compete for that phrase and gives you an analysis rating of your chances of getting a high ranking page for the keywords you are considering.

You can also use their misspellings tool which takes popular words and shows you common misspellings so you can incorporate those misspellings into your Meta tags to get additional traffic.

Several subscription options allow you to access their databases from around $5 per day to $90 for 3 months. Well worth every penny if you plan to promote products on the Internet. See **wordtracker.com**.

Alexa

While we're on the subject of research, a great addition to your Web browser is Alexa. Alexa is a free Web navigation service that works with your browser to provide essential information about each site you visit. It appears in its own window on your desktop and goes with you while you are browsing the net.

Find out how your site measures up to the competition in popularity. Find related sites. A very useful reference and it's free at: **www.alexa.com**.

Autoresponders

Autoresponders are email addresses which automatically reply to messages with a standard reply, greeting or marketing message. An example is that you might want the address info@yourdomain.com to automatically reply with a preformatted message with prices, information, or a thank you note. Some Web hosting services charge for autoresponders, but others provide them for free. See the chapter on email for sources.

Database management

A database program manages records organized by subjects into categories called fields. Example uses include keeping customer contact information and sales history, supplier information, tracking Web sites you have sought links from, and accounting records for your expenses and income.

Microsoft Access and **FileMaker Pro** are examples of database management software. You can find these or others at computer stores or purchase from online sellers. Both Access and FileMaker Pro are easy to learn and provide numerous import and export functions for moving data to and from other software programs.

Secure server for online shopping

If you are going to allow for customers to purchase online at your site, consider providing a secure server option through your Web host. If you don't know whether your host offers secure server, contact them directly.

Netscape Navigator and Microsoft Internet Explorer, encrypt transactions using Secure Sockets Layer (SSL), a process that allows a secure connection to the server. This encrypts and protects the information as it travels over the Internet.

You know that a Web site is secured by SSL is when the URL begins with "https:" instead of "http :" and a small icon of a lock or an unbroken key appears on the screen of the browser, usually in the lower left.

Hosting services which provide SSL cost a little more, but that small amount will be one more guarantee of safety that helps customers make the purchase decision. For sources of Web hosts, see the appendix.

Taking Orders Online

In order for your customers to make a purchase directly from your Web site, you may want a shopping cart page(s) or a link to a shopping cart located elsewhere. Many Web hosts provide the option of having a cart with your site for an extra monthly fee.

Many online malls offer shopping cart with a storefront. Usually, these carts are not very customizable. Third party shopping cart services offer another alternative. ShopCart at **www.shopcart.com** offers their cart service for around $35 a month.

Another option is providing a form that the customer can fill in online. When the customer is finished, she hits a "submit" button which sends the customer's order to you by email.

You can locate programs for creating forms by searching for "mail order forms". The problem with using these simple forms to take orders is that if you offer several products that customers are likely to buy in quantity, the forms usually can't total the purchase, add sales tax and verify the credit card like most shopping carts.

Accept credit cards

Merchant account status with your bank or similar organization allows you to accept popular credit cards like Mastercard, Visa, Discover and American Express. Being capable of accepting credit cards is essential for retail sales online.

If you don't have merchant account status, there are several companies that will act as brokers to help you gain such an account. There are other companies online that will allow you to use their merchant status and charge you a commission for each sale that is processed by you.

Amazon.com has created a program called zshops. Through their "One-Click" option, Amazon uses their merchant status to allow buyers to purchase from you with their credit cards for which you pay a small commission - around 5% of the sale.

Examples of other service providers online for accepting credit cards can be reviewed from:

www.craftmarketer.com/accepting_credit_cards.htm

Another option is PayPal, a service that allows a variety of online payment options for personal and business use. There is no sign up fee and the commission paid to PayPal for business transactions is less than a typical credit card commission. For details, visit: **www.PayPal.com** .

If you search for the term "accept credit cards," you'll get many listings. However, be sure to thoroughly investigate any company before entering into an agreement.

Search engine submission services and software

In general, submit your pages by hand to the top ten search engines because these engines are those most used by the online audience. The reason for submitting by hand is that some submission programs and services botch your submission by not keeping up to date with every search engine submission requirements. You cannot risk missing listings.

Web Position, mentioned earlier, also submits your pages to the major engines effectively. See the chapter on search engines for submission tips. A free site that submits your URL to 30 major search engines is **www.addme.com**.

Search Engine Watch subscription

Search Engine Watch is an invaluable Web site which offers the latest news about search engines. A site subscription provides access to detailed information about all the major search engines, including submission tips, writing META tags, etc.

Subscribers also receive an exclusive email newsletter twice per month. This site offers both free information and more advanced reports for around $60 a year - **www.SearchEngineWatch.com.**

Research software

One of the best tools I have found for researching any topic, especially my keywords, is a program called Copernic. Copernic searches several of the best search engines, discussion groups, newsgroups and many other sites on the Internet. After the search is complete, Copernic can display the findings in a catalog type browser window allowing you to visit and check out each finding. Best news is that Copernic is free at **www.copernic.com**. Another useful and free software search program is Bulls Eye at **www.intelliseek.com**.

Skills needed . . .

Experience on how to use a computer

This book does not teach basic computer skills, but it does prepare you for successful marketing online. There are plenty of beginner computer guides in your local bookstore. You can find a good source for new user information at:

www.newbieclub.com/?learnaboutcomputers

     After you know how to use your computer's operating system, you want to be able to go back and forth among the different software programs you will be using in your business. Examples of programs you will want in your business include: accounting, database, spreadsheet, word processor, page layout, Internet browser, Web page composer, and image manager.

     You should be familiar with how to load software onto your computer and how to manage your files. Organize files you create like you would documents in a filing cabinet. Keep separate file folders for your documents outside of the programs these documents are created with. For instance, if you regularly type a letter of welcome to a new customer, file it in a folder called "letters."

     If you don't have experience in the above, there are probably local user groups in your community where you can get help learning basic skills. You can also find help online by going to a directory like Yahoo and searching for "database tutorial" or "spreadsheet tutorial" or whatever topic you wish to learn about.

Familiarity with sending, receiving and managing email

     Email is your basic electronic mail and should be considered your most important means of contacting your customers. In addition to "Thank you" notes, you will want to create follow up emails to send to new customers to keep your name in front of them on a regular basis. The free programs for managing email, Pegasus and Eudora will speed the process.

Ability to surf the Internet and use search engines

     Search engines are the top way of bringing traffic your site. Therefore, you should learn everything you can about how they work. Read and reread the chapter on search engines and subscribe to the free newsletters listed in the appendix.

Web site design and maintenance

There are at least two ways to get your site built. Do it yourself or hire someone to build it for you. The problem with hiring someone is that you will want to make regular changes and updates for which they will usually charge you. The advantage of hiring the design out is that it frees you to concentrate on marketing and promotion.

With plenty of advanced and affordable software available, I recommend you consider learning to design a Web site yourself. Even if you later decide to hire a "professional" Web designer to spruce up the look and feel of your site, you will gain invaluable insights by learning how a commercial site should function. See the chapter on building a Web site that sells for help when designing your site. Also, see the book *Poor Richard's Web Site* by Peter Kent.

Underneath all the visible elements on your site, lies the hidden language of Web page design, HTML (Hyper-Text Mark-up Language.)

If the idea of learning programming code is intimidating, relax. HTML is relatively easy to learn and manipulate. Best of all, you can learn or copy almost everything you will need to know for free on the Internet. Here are some of the best sites that teach HTML. For more sites, see the Appendix or do a search for "learn HTML" and you'll soon have enough material to be an expert.

davecentral.com
www.htmlgoodies.earthweb.com
www.gazoo.net/htmhell
www.cwru.edu/help/introHTML/toc.html
www.hotwired.com/webmonkey/teachingtool

Patience and persistence

The Internet can seem overwhelming. Learning to market your product online can be even more challenging. It may take three months to a year to see results, depending on how much time you can afford to invest. Many people give up too soon and all the previous work is for nothing. Hang in there and keep following the marketing plan outlined later in this guide.

Chapter 3 Where to Host Your Site

Web sites are located at Web hosts who usually collect monthly rental fees for the service. Finding a Web site is similar to renting an apartment inside a large complex.

There are several kinds of hosting services for your business. Many of the national ISP's offer a personal page when you sign up for their Internet service. Other options include free Web sites at numerous spots on the net, your site within an online mall, as a subdirectory under another domain, or at a host site with your own domain name.

Of all the choices, getting your own domain site offers the most benefits for a craft business. However, you may want to consider all the options described in this chapter to increase your Web presence for purposes of creating links to your main site and adding more pages to the search engines.

Your domain name at a Web host

Your own domain on a Web host is the most useful scenario for marketing online. Going this avenue is usually cheaper than getting involved with an online mall or trying to run your own server which is complicated and time consuming.

I pay $49 a month for a domain Web site package that includes 12 POP3 email accounts, SSL, cgi-bin, Mysql database, shopping cart, unlimited autoresponders and a host of other goodies for doing commerce online. If you are interested in more details on my host, please send an email request to **james@craftmarketer.com** and say you want more information on Web hosting.

When you register a domain at **www.networksolutions.com**, you own the address, no matter where you move your site. If you go with one of the other registering services, be careful to read their agreement terms. Those services offering free or low cost domain names may have written in fine print that they, not you, own the domain name, which is useless to you. In these situations, if you are not happy with the host you are with, and you decide to host your site elsewhere, you lose all the traffic you have built up.

When you own the domain, you can go elsewhere and take the URL of your Web site with you, thus continuing to benefit from your promotions efforts. Since the domain name is where people point their browsers to, traffic goes to that address no matter where you host the site - assuming your host is up and running.

With your own domain name, you don't have to reprint your business cards or brochures should you change hosts.

Typically, you get your domain name around the time you find your Web host. However, you can reserve a domain name for two years without having a host for an extra fee at **NetworkSolutions.com**.

Pages on ISP's

If you signed up with an ISP like AOL, you were given a personal Web page with several megabytes capacity for storing your page(s). For instance, your AOL personal page would be accessed by visitors at members.aol.com/yourwebpageaddress. Your cost involved is only what you pay for your monthly Internet service, probably around $20 a month.

The problem with using this kind of address for running a business is that the ISP domain address conveys the impression that you didn't have the money to get your own domain name so you went with a cheaper option. The personal pages on ISP's may be fine for fun but are not in your best interests if you are trying to gain customer confidence.

In addition to giving the appearance that you cannot afford your own domain, ISP's personal pages rarely offer you the commercial options you need for running a business. For example, you would not have the ability to put up a shopping cart on a secured server at an AOL personal page.

Many of the larger ISP's do offer commercial site hosting in addition to Internet access with accompanying personal pages. Their fees tend to be higher than independent Web hosting services.

Free pages

Many sites allow you to put up Web pages at no charge. Design options are limited, and as with the ISP personal pages, you get an address at the Web host's domain, not your own. If you have limited funds for putting up your site, the sites listed below will give you free pages. Again, the impression you give by hosting at another domain other than your own is unfavorable for business purposes. Also, you may have difficulty getting your pages on these sites listed with search engines because of anti-SPAM filters. SPAMers tend to use one free service after another, because once the complaints against them begin, they are shut down and have to move on. See:

www.angelfire.lycos.com
www.free.com
www.freemerchant.com
www.freehomepage.com
www.geocities.yahoo.com
www.rubylane.com
www.tripod.lycos.com

For additional sites that provide free Web pages, so a search for "free web hosting" or "free web pages" at any major search engine.

Online malls/galleries

There are many shopping malls online who actively solicit small businesses to rent space within their domain. Most of them claim their promotional marketing brings visitors to the mall who will wander through the sites including yours. However, independent studies show most visitors find sites through search engines while few people arrive through a mall's directory.

There are an abundance of craft selling malls and galleries online. Should you join one? Except for one gallery owner who told me she was so satisfied with results in an online gallery that she set up her own Web site, most craft persons in online malls say they are disappointed in their mall sales.

Larger malls, like iMall.com offer Web page templates which make it easy to set up your site. They also provide shopping cart options and accept credit card payments for you. For all of these services, you pay a range of fees depending on your program.

You should not rely on the mall to generate traffic to your storefront but rather on your own independent promotional efforts. An online gallery with specific kinds of art or craft will have an advantage because of the ability to promote to niche audiences and draw targeted buyers.

One major disadvantage of setting up in an online mall is that search engines may not list your pages located at the mall's Web site. However, one way around the search engine block would be to have a domain name Web site that linked back to your mall page.

An advantage worth considering is that an online mall may be able to design a good looking site for you at a reasonable price. This is good if you don't have time to design a site yourself. Remember however, the mall is going to make money off you from your setup fees, monthly rental charges, sales commissions and design charges whether you make any sales or not.

If you desire to check out what online malls for arts and crafts may provide, visit the links page at

www.craftmarketer.com/links/themeindex.html

Look for the link pointing to "Craft Malls and Galleries."

If you decide to get involved in an online mall, you should ask these questions:

• Does the mall produce enough traffic to justify costs?

• Is a shopping cart option with ability to accept major credit cards available?

• Are you allowed to advertise your mall page's address outside of the mall? In other words, if you list your address at the mall's domain will visitors be taken directly to your site or are they forced to go through the mall's home page?

• Does the mall charge a flat monthly fee or do they also ask for a percentage of each sale?

• Contact at least a dozen other participants in the mall and ask them about their experiences.

Something between having a storefront and an online mall with no setup fees or monthly charges is at Ruby Lane website at **www.rubylane.com**. The only fee to you is a commission charged when you make the sale.

Chapter 4   How to Design a Web Site That Sells

It may seem obvious that you need a Web site before you can promote it. Bear in mind that the methods you use to get traffic to your Web site will be influenced by some of the functions you include when building your site. For instance, you might include a form page for visitors to give you their email addresses in order to get on your newsletter list. You can then use your newsletter to promote pages on your Web site again and again.

It's quite possible to put up a simple Web site in a few days. Then, over the next few months, you may go back and forth between designing and marketing your Web site until you fine tune its functions to do what it's meant to do — sell your craftwork.

Design your site so that as visitors navigate through the Web pages, the path they take leads them to do what you want, which is in many cases, to buy your craft products. If your site's pages allows them to wander in many directions, either on your site or to other Web sites, they will do just that.

You must also have clear and consistent navigation throughout the site. An underlying design theme throughout every page conveys a professional image to your visitors.

Provide step-by-step instructions. Use simple language. Compose your text as if you were addressing an audience at the eighth grade level which is considered to be the average reader's comprehension.

Define your purpose

If you don't know what your site is for, your visitors certainly won't either. This may sound obvious, but you would be surprised how many commercial sites are out there that look like they have no clear purpose.

When I browse the Web for sources of information or products, I come across about one out of every ten sites which is useless. Do you think I hang around long enough to figure out how to get what

I want? No, I go on. So do you and almost everyone else who is surfing the net.

Before you go any further in thoughts about your site's appearance, define the unique selling proposition. This is not that difficult because in most cases what you are selling is your craft product.

In addition to creating a site that clearly shows visitors what it's purpose is, a successful site should feature:

- interactive catalog of products/services you sell or offer.
- automated shipping and tracking.
- a secure system to record and verify credit card orders.
- several means by which customers can contact you, like email, toll free number, fax, and mailing address.

Design your site for fast loading

If your site takes a long time to download, you will lose visitors. One of the culprits for slow loading pages is large graphic images. Other villains that will slow your site loading are frames, animations, audio files, video files and complex java scripts.

Eventually, everyone will have access to broadband access which allows more data to move faster, including voice and video. Until that time, eliminate all of these fancy gimmicks. They won't increase your site's traffic and will probably deter visitors with older browser versions from hanging around long enough for the site to load. Older versions of browsers sometimes can't read the latest Web design files if they are created with newer technology.

Optimizing graphic images

The following is a list of online resources for optimizing your graphics for smaller size and fast loading:

Gif Lube (free image optimizer online) - **websitegarage.netscape.com/P=ref30d32e55/O=wsg/ turbocharge/gif_lube/index.html**

NetMechanic Image Optimization (free image optimizer online) - **www.netmechanic.com/accelerate.htm**

JPEG Wizard -
www.webreference.com/services/graphics/jw

Spin Wave - **www.spinwave.com** (free trial download).

You can also get the ability to compress graphics in the better photo software programs. Adobe Photoshop's latest version offers good compression features. **www.adobe.com**.

ULoad Smartsaver at **www.webutilities.com/products/SSPro/runme.htm** - free trial download.

Web Graphics Optimizer at **WebOpt.com** - free trial download.

WebFX allows you to create special effects and vary the compression size of Web graphics. This free online tool is at **nbswebfx.com**

Some Web design programs allow you to quickly produce a "thumbnail" of your photo images. This feature creates a smaller thumbnail image of your full size images.

Thumbnail images download very fast compared to full size pictures. When someone clicks on the thumbnail, the full size image pops up. The full size image is not a Web page, but an image file displayed in the browser.

You could manually create a separate page for the larger image. This separate page would be able to have its own META tags and page title which you can post to the search engines and thus increase your odds of getting seen since most search engines will spider most of your site's pages.

META tags

When constructing your Web pages, pay attention to META tags. A META tag or variable adds information to the header for a page. You do not see the META tags except when you are looking at the HTML code of your page. This variable corresponds to the "name" attribute in the META tag and is not visible to site visitors unless they go to "view page source" on their browser.

META tags are special instructions to a Web browser, such as a description, a set of keywords, an expiration date, a copyright or a display-refresh value.

Names for META variables look like this in HTML:

```
<title>Fashion accessories handwoven by James
Dillehay</title>
<meta name="DESCRIPTION" content="Fashion
accessory handmade wearable art and southwestern
rugs by weaving fiber artist, James Dillehay">
<meta name="KEYWORDS" content="fashion
accessory,shawl,handmade gift,wearable art,
southwestern rug, handwoven, weaving, scarf">
```

The most important META tags are the Title, Description and Keywords because you can include your important keywords in these areas. META tags, however, do not count as much in search engine rankings as they once did, but there are other reasons to include them. Notably, your description META tag may be the content that shows up on a search results page. Also, you can include misspellings of your keywords in the keywords META tags.

For a useful overview of META tags, see **searchenginewatch.com/meta.htm**.

The keyword META tag is a list of your keywords separated by commas. Some search engines will only count so many characters including spaces as keywords when they spider pages. If you don't leave a space after each comma, you get more characters or keywords counted.

Be sure to use META tags in the header of each page. Each page should have the keywords present on that page in the META tags. In other words, don't use the same set of keywords in all your pages' META tags.

Search engines change the way they search and score sites because they want sites ranked on content and popularity. They know Web designers cheat so they constantly look for ways to identify tricks.

In general, avoid using your most important keywords more than three times in META tags. If you try to load the META tags with more repetitions of keywords, they interpret this as SPAM and they may disregard the page.

META information is used by many search engines, and can affect the way your site is listed. AltaVista, for example, will use the first 30 words it finds on your visible Web page for a description unless you have included a META description tag. If you provide a META description, the engine will quote from that tag and display your description on the search results page. Some search engines ignore META tags, but enough access them to make it worth your while to include them on each page.

Design tips for higher search engine rankings

There are several ways you can improve your placement in the search engines. If the techniques seem confusing, go to the HTML tutorials mentioned earlier or visit **searchenginewatch.com** for an overview.

• Your keywords should appear near the top of a Web page in the heading and in the first few paragraphs of text. Keywords that appear near the beginning of a paragraph and near the end of a paragraph result in "keyword prominence" which helps your ranking.

• A search engine measures how often keywords appear in relation to other words in a Web page. Keywords appearing more frequently throughout the page are seen as more relevant than other Web pages, up to a certain point. The job of designing your pages for higher ranking in the engines is made easier with **Web Position**. Keyword frequency ratio is different for each engine and Web Position stays up to date with the changes and upgrades itself regularly.

• Search engines cannot browse or index images. Therefore, use what is known as the ALT attribute in HTML image tags to include text which the engines will index. For example:

<IMG BORDER = "0" SRC = "glass_angel.jpg" ALT = "stained glass angel">

In the example, the glass_angel.jpg image does not get read by the search engines, but the ALT text "stained glass angel" does, thus giving you additional keyword use which boosts your ranking.

• Find a site that scores highly based on a search using your important keywords at one of the top search engines. In your browser's menu bar, you have the option of viewing a Web page's source or HTML code. View the source code for the top ranking sites and note which keywords are used in the META tags. Using these same keywords may help get your page a higher ranking at that same engine.

• Include your keywords in the page title.

• Use many shorter pages instead of one long page. Each page with its different META tags, page titles, and keyword rich text will boost your odds of getting a page to appear when someone is doing a search.

• Avoid creating duplicate pages with the same META tags or text content because some engines, especially AltaVista, now interpret duplicate pages as an attempt to fool the engine.

Design your site for viewing in different browsers

Netscape Navigator and Internet Explorer somehow interpret HTML code in different ways. The result is that your carefully designed site may appear fine in one browser but look askew in another. The solution is to see how your site appears under all conditions. You can keep a version of both browsers on your system or you can use a Web tool for viewing pages as all browsers see them. Check out Delorie.com which lets you see your site under varying conditions at **www.delorie.com**.

You may also want to look at what software programs can accomplish for maximizing your HTML code. HTML Power Tools, at **www.tali.com**, is a software that can customize your site for a particular browser, check your HTML code for errors, check broken links and other tasks that might be time consuming if done by hand.

Make the site interactive

Get customers to buy by encouraging them to linger on your site or return to it enough to realize what you are selling. Below are several ways to get visitors to interact with your site. The more they view your products, the closer they get to purchasing.

Many of the interactive tools will also allow you to capture your visitors contact information, especially emails. Read more about the importance of building a contact list in Chapter 8, Promoting Through Email.

You want quick and easy ways to get email addresses. Visitors to your site must take some action in order for you to capture their address. Since they may have some resistance to giving you their information, you have to make the process simple and painless. Here's the easiest way I've seen.

You can create a button that requires a simple click and motivates action. Clicking on the button sends you their email address and probably their user name.

The following HTML simple code creates a button on your site.

```
<FORMMETHOD="post"ACTION="mailto:youremail@yourdomain.com?
subject=IncomingFromClick">
<INPUT TYPE="submit" VALUE="Click here">
</FORM>
```

This code works on your page when you replace youremail@yourdomain.com with your own email address. You can also have any text on the button you want by replacing "Click here" with your choice. Where it says "IncomingFromClick" is what appears in the subject of the email message going to you, so you can change that to whatever you wish.

Why would anyone click on your button? You can have many incentives to get them to do so. You could let them know that clicking is to their benefit by saying something like: "Click here to receive updates. Your address will never be given to another party."

You could also offer them something free like a catalog, free report or a sample of your product. When you offer a free item, announce it with a press release to get free publicity. Editors are always looking for services for their readers. See Chapter 10 on getting and using publicity to promote site traffic.

Also you can announce your free item on these Web sites:

www.download.com
www.thefreesite.com
www.free-stuff.com
www.free2try.com
www.freehound.com
www.free-sweepstakes.com
www.huronline.com
www.freecontests.com

Free classified ads

Set up a classified ad section where visitors can post classifieds for free. There are several types of software packages that automate the process of receiving and posting ads. See more about setting up classifieds section on your site in Chapter 13 on advertising.

Contests

Operating a contest online provides several benefits:
• You capture contact information from contestants.
• Contestants who enter return to check their status.
• Contests generate word-of-mouth referrals bringing in others.
• You draw attention to your products.

An example of an online contest is called *Find the Double.*

Somewhere on your Web site you include the same product twice. Those who enter the contest have to read your entire product listing to discover which product is shown two times.

Setting up this kind of contest guarantees your products will get looked at because visitors view all of your products.

You might run the contest for a period of time like a week and then select the winner. When choosing the prize, give some product or service that indicates the winner has an interest in what you provide. For instance, if your site promotes historical wood carving techniques, you might give away a free booklet explaining the craft. The booklet should also include a flyer on your Web site's products.

The significant part of the contest is how you follow-up when it's over. Send all the contestants an email announcing and congratulating the winner. In the same email, you want to promote your art or craft products. This follow up is the end you want to achieve when you begin the contest. The contest created a means to collect email addresses of prospects so you can do a direct email announcement to them offering your work for sale.

You also achieved the result of getting prospects to view your work online when they searched for the double listing.

Using holidays and special occasions

You could create a new Web page whenever a holiday is approaching. Update your site at least one month before every holiday.

Find out interesting facts about each special occasion and post the information to your page. Your special occasion page can also feature how your art or craft items related to that day.

For instance, you could post a report on the origin of Christmas or how Christmas is celebrated in 33 countries. Randomly place your Christmas related items throughout the text with links to your shopping cart. Be sure to include a "click here" under each image.

A birthday list of gemstones could accompany jewelry items set with the individual stones along with a description of the stone's special characteristics.

Flower essences lend themselves to folklore and fairies. You could have a lot of fun weaving fantasy into crafts and get more visitor interaction.

Add a discussion group to your site

If the subject of your craft is of interest to enough people, they may be interested in joining a discussion group you set up on your Web site. Setting up a discussion group page is not difficult. FrontPage has a template that creates one for you in minutes.

The way discussion pages work, participants can enter comments and questions via an interactive form on a discussion page. The webmaster or moderator (probably you) monitors the comments to keep out advertisers and pornographers.

The first few words of each comment shows up in an outline format allowing other visitors to click on the comment and read the full message. Replies to comments are indented under the respective comments so that the page looks like a table of contents.

Survey of what makes a customers buy online

What turns a visitor into a paying customer? Here's what one successful Web site owner found out about his site by polling his customers (multiple responses brought rates for percentages shown.)

69% liked the look of the site

42% site had biggest selection

39% contained more information than other sites

37% found that what they needed was listed

32% Web site was easy to use

31% product was on hand & available for immediate delivery

21% product photos were top quality

18% offer of free shipping

15% competitive pricing

11% top ranking when appeared in the search engine

6% existing customers

5% word of mouth referrals

How to get customers to refer others

Word of mouth referrals from customers who like your work, cost you nothing while helping you build your customer base. People who like you or your work are usually enthusiastic when telling others, often making a sale for you without realizing they were selling.

Many companies have begun to look at referral incentives to increase their business. Network marketing companies thrive on referrals. People listen to friends they trust. You can create an easy referral system on your Web site, by utilizing a free program at **www.letemknow.com**. Of course, you will want your Web site to be fine tuned and easy to navigate before you start asking others to send their friends.

A good way of getting new business is to offer a discount or gift certificate to customers who refer others. Create a code number for the gift certificate that you can track. Put a time limitation on the offer to encourage the customer to act now.

Instill customer confidence

Your Web site should make the visitor feel that you are a legitimate business which stands behind its work and will deliver as promised. Ways of creating confidence include:

• Listing a toll free number on every page. If you don't have a toll free number for customers to order by and want to bypass the expensive rates from ATT, you can get an 800, 888, or 877 number at 4.9 cents per minute, a small monthly service charge and no set-up fee. The service is described in detail at

www.maktrix.com/toll-free-numbers.htm

• List your regular phone number for persons calling from outside the U.S.. Shortly after including this information on my shopping cart, I received a call from Italy for a product order.

• Include an alternative order page for those who would rather call, mail or fax in an order.

• Get the ability to accept major credit cards. Include graphic logos from these cards on your Web pages - Mastercard, Visa, Discover, American Express - because everyone knows these are trustworthy companies to deal with. If you are associated with them, you get more of that trust.

• Provide access to a secured server for credit card transactions.

• Create a site that is fast to download and easy to navigate. For craft artists this means clear photos of your work that loads quickly. Your customer knows you care about his/her time enough to make your site user friendly.

• Don't make it difficult to do business with you, or to contact you. List several ways of reaching you like your toll free number, contact email address, fax, phone, postal address and alternatives to online ordering.

• State the length of your guarantee. The longer you provide a guarantee, the more confidence the customer feels in ordering. A longer guarantee time makes it less likely someone will actually request a return.

Follow these simple rules as you conduct your online business. Put the confidence builders on every single Web page. People will sense your fairness and honesty. They will like you, and when people like you, they will become repeat customers.

Take your tips from the winning Web sites

Several businesses have brought in millions of dollars in sales from their Web sites, like **Amazon.com**. Amazon may have had problems showing a profit, but they know how to make sales. Their revenues in 1999 were over $1.5 billion.

Study the Web pages of Amazon.com and **1800Flowers.com**. To see how they turn visitors into buyers, look at their online shopping cart, ease of site navigation, fast loading pages and secure server for accepting credit cards.

Online storefronts

When you don't have much time for Web site design but just want to get your business online and running as quickly as possible, check out the following ecommerce site packages. For a variety of prices ranging from free to hefty monthly service fees, you can get your business and products online about as fast as you can type.

Services include design, catalog, domain registration, credit card merchant account and more, all in a package deal. A few providers include: **www.virtualave.net**, **www.bigstep.com**, and **store.yahoo.com**

Sample Web page

The Web page below is one of my pages for selling my fiber art. You can view this page online at **www.craftmarketer.com/ fashion_accessory.htm**.

Fashion Accessory Clothing

Southwestern Rugs

Handmade gifts woven by James Dillehay, fiber artist, Torreon, New Mexico. Inspired by the enchanting high mountain deserts of New Mexico, these handmade clothes will delight and please your senses.

100% Cotton Ruana - $150 **purchase now**

Southwestern rugs hand loomed from 100% pure virgin wool. Sturdy construction promises you years of enjoyable use.

Desert Rainbow 36" x 60" 100% virgin wool. $750 **purchase now**

click on photos for full size image

Wool/mohair sweater $165 **purchase now**

Woven by loom using only the finest natural yarns like virgin wool and angora mohair, Dillehay's wearable art is soft as snow and warms you on cool days.

[home]
[free web hosting]
[free report on high ranking web pages]
[speed up internet connection]

How to contact us:

James Dillehay, Fiber Artist
P.O. Box 75, Torreon NM 87061
For orders, call (800)235-6570
Fax: (603)388-8076
*Email: **James@craftmarketer.com***

Gathering of Tribes 24" x 60" $500

Sample HTML source code

Here is part of the HTML source code for the previous page.

```html
<html>
<head>
<title>Fashion accessories handwoven by James Dillehay</title>
<meta name="DESCRIPTION" content="Fashion accessory handmade wearable
art and southwestern rugs by weaving fiber artist, James Dillehay">
<meta name="KEYWORDS" content="fashion accessory,shawl,handmade
gift,wearable art,southwestern rug,handwoven,weaving,scarf,James Dillehay">
<meta http-equiv="Content-Language" content="en-us">
<meta http-equiv="Content-Type" content="text/html; charset=windows-1252">
</head>
<body>
<!—fashion accessory,wearable art,southwestern rug,handmade
gift,shawl,scarf—>
<div align="center">
 <center>
 <table border="0" cellpadding="2" cellspacing="4" width="613">
   <tr>
   <td valign="top" align="center" width="98"><br><br><br><br><img border="0"
src="images/black_ruana_small.jpg" alt="fashion accessory - hand made
clothing" width="90" height="134">
     <p><font size="1">100% Cotton Ruana - $150</font></p>
     </td>
   </center>
    <td width="267" valign="top" align="center">
    <h3 align="left">Fashion Accessory Clothing</h3>
    <p align="left">Handmade gifts woven by James Dillehay, fiber artist,
Torreon, New Mexico.</p>
    <p align="left">Inspired by the enchanting high mountain<img border="0"
src="images/james_oval_copy.JPG" align="right" width="60" height="78"
alt="Southwestern rug weavings by James Dillehay"> deserts of New 
Mexico, the handmade clothing of weaver, James Dillehay, will delight and please
your senses.</p>
    <p align="left"><font size="1"><i>click on photo for full size image</i></
font></p>
    <p align="left"><a href="2girls.jpg"><img border="2" src="2girls_small.jpg"
alt="wearable art - handmade clothing" width="100" height="89"></a>
    <font size="1">Wool/mohair sweater $165</font></p>
  <center>
    </center><p align="left">Woven by loom using only the finest natural yarns
like virgin wool and angora mohair, Dillehay's wearable art is soft as snow and
warms you on cool days.</p>
    </td>
    <td valign="top" align="center" width="214"><h3 align="left">Southwestern
Rugs</h3>
    <p align="left">Southwestern rugs hand loomed from 100% pure virgin wool.
Sturdy construction promises you years of enjoyable use.</p>
    <p align="left"><a href="rainbow.jpg"><img border="2"
src="rainbow_small.jpg" alt="Southwestern rug" align="right" width="100"
height="142"></a></p>
    <p align="center"><font size="1"><b><i>Desert Rainbow</i></b><br>
```

Checklist for creating a Web site

Tasks for Stage 1 - First steps	Due Date	Done Date
Establish a budget of how much you can afford to spend to create, host, maintain and promote a web site.		
Decide if you will design your site or hire someone else. Get quotes from several sources and ask for examples of previous work.		
Determine the purpose of your site. For many of us the goal is generating sales and leads.		
Check out other sites similar in subject matter.		
Learn to use search engines for research.		
Get a dial-up account with an Internet Service Provider. (Don't use AOL or Compuserve for your main business account.)		
Come up with an eight word title, a twenty-five word description and twenty-five keywords that best describe your site.		
Create a file for your graphic images, logos and text blocks that will make up your site's content. Gather all your material.		
Check out the free sites for learning about web site design. (see Appendix)		

Tasks for Stage 2 - Creating the web site	Due Date	Don Date
Decide when your site wil be ready.		
Determine your domain name.		
Find a web host. At the time you register your domain name you will need to get an account with a web host.		
If using a designer to build your site, meet and plan the project. Make all graphics and text material available to the designer.		
If you are designing the site yourself, visit at least a dozen sites to look at examples of navigation and lay-out.		
Create a flow chart on paper of how your web pages should be organized. List links, images, text, navigation bars, discussion pages, fill-in forms and shopping cart.		
If you have graphic files, convert them to JPEG or GIF formats and compress them for fast loading.		
Create your web pages. Use FrontPage, PageMill or another web authoring software.		
When your pages are complete, run a spell check and verify all links.		

Tasks for Stage 3 - Fine tuning META tags	Due Date	Done Date
Create each page to have a unique page title in the HTML code containing your keywords		
Check each page for use of keywords in content.		
Check each page for including keywords in META keywords tag		
Check each page for META description tag. Include keywords in description.		
Check images for use of ALT text which should include your keywords.		
Optimize your web pages to rank high in major search engines with Web Position software .Free trial download of Web Position at http://www.craftmarketer.com/web-position-software.htm		

Tasks for Stage 4 - Publishing the web site	Due Date	Done Date
Have friends check out your site and tell you what they think when moving through it. Have them check links to see if they lead where they are supposed to.		
Publish (upload) your pages to your web site.		
Test your links, emails, interactive forms, shopping cart to see if eveything is working.		
Begin promotional activities.		

Chapter 5 How to Succeed With a Marketing Plan

A marketing plan helps you learn who your customers are and how they will find you, A plan helps you get to think like they do. Putting yourself in the shoes of your customer is critical in any business plan, but even more important on the Internet.

I know many craft artists who never give much thought to marketing or planning. They just do the shows or get their store accounts and go along merrily until trends change. Suddenly, no one is buying their work and they don't know what to do. With a little time spent planning, one can determine several viable markets for sales. If one avenue slows down, you have other options for staying afloat.

Answering the following questions will help you begin thinking about an Internet marketing plan.

• What does your site do? What is the main benefit to your visitor? Do you want it to educate, entertain or sell? Do you want to create new prospects or stay in touch with regular customers? Do you want to attract more wholesale buyers? Are you looking for international buyers?

• Who is most likely to be your customer? What type of person is she/he? Example: age, sex, income level, education. Give serious thought to determining who are the visitors to your site(s). This is a big part of learning how it should be designed. You may have more than one type of visitor. For example, you may have U.S. retail customers, wholesale customers, catalog buyers, and international buyers.

• What other kinds of sites are your visitors likely to visit? For instance, if you sell quilts, people visiting your site might also be reached through Web sites about sewing. Visitors should be able to:
  • interact with your site
  • leave their contact information
  • purchase something you are selling
  • refer others to you

You will feel less confused when you market your Web site in stages. That is, create targeted goals and measure the results you get whenever you complete a phase. By working in measurable steps, you can pace yourself and track which efforts are worth pursuing further and which activities you should abandon. If you don't work in stages, you will find yourself overwhelmed, scattered and consequently disappointed in the whole process.

Setting up a work flow plan

"Work flow" means how the steps in your plan follow each other from one to the next. In other words, what do you do first, then second, third and so on. The following list shows a very simple work flow organization for promoting your craft through a Web site:

• First, write down 15 to 30 keywords and phrases that persons might use in searches to find your site.

• Next, visit **www.WordTracker.com** and learn how many searches are done for each of your keywords.

• Design your Web pages to rank high for those keywords.

• Submit your pages to the search engines.

• Track your results frequently.

• Redesign and resubmit until you are regularly achieving high rankings in the major engines.

Organize your work flow so that you can accomplish tasks in a focused and effective way. Later in this chapter, you will see example forms you can reproduce and modify to help you track your activities for each Web related marketing task.

You could also create more detailed work flow sheets for specific tasks like seeking links from other sites, writing articles and news releases, setting up auctions and any group of tasks that require organized, daily action steps.

What a Web site is going to cost you

The cost of setting up to market on the Internet can range from almost free to several thousand dollars. This book gives you many resources for free options like free Web hosting, free ISP, free design help and other no cost services.

Free isn't always better in trying to establish credibility as a business that inspires customer confidence to make a purchase from you. You can certainly find reliable Web hosts for around $25 a month that will host your domain name. That's not a bad price for a 24 hour advertising vehicle.

After the Web hosting issue is resolved, you will want to invest in a few minimum software programs to speed your page publishing and getting higher rankings in the search engines. I recommend several programs throughout this guide that have helped me achieve high ranking pages and track my promotions for an investment of under $500. Still not bad for a business expense when you compare what it would cost you to drive out of state to a craft fair.

The biggest challenge in determining your costs will probably revolve around whether you design and promote your site yourself or hire someone to help. Hiring a Web page designer can get costly. As much as possible, take advantage of the free resources listed in the appendix before you spend money on a designer. If you have invested in costly Web site design, you are going to have expectations about returns in the form of revenues that just simply may not happen until you generate traffic and sales.

How much will you earn?

Can you ever be certain of what you will earn when you go to a craft show? Even shows that are good year after year can one day turn into losers. There is no way to predict how profitable your site will be until you put it up and announce it. Even then, in most cases, it may take several months to obtain measurable results.

Those Web sites that are making sales usually have common characteristics like products offered on the site are products people want to buy, prices of the products are competitive, the site has traffic coming in on a regular basis, visitors are motivated to look around the site once they arrive, and the owner of the Web site looks reputable.

The other requirement of success for a small business owner including artisans is to target defined niche audiences, such as persons who collect hand made work or persons shopping for gifts.

The marketing value of the Internet is its ability to locate and cater to groups of interest within groups of interest. The original use of the Internet was scientific and educational research coordinated by special interest. That purpose eventually led to the development of targeting specific markets for commercial means by businesses.

After a few months, take your average number of visitors and divide your sales by this number. The result will be the average value of each visitor. The next step is to increase the number of visitors, that is, the kind of visitors who are most interested in your work. Experiment slightly with page design to see if one offer results in more purchases than other offers.

Just as you get better at predicting your offline sales after you have been in business for a year, you will become more accurate at projecting your Internet income.

Creating a marketing plan

The following checklists will help you get started in planning to market your craft products over the Internet. As your business grows, you will create your own checklists. The lists here will give you plenty to begin with.

Do not let the order in which the tasks are listed stop you from taking an action step to get another promotion going right away. The purpose of the lists is to provide a focused approach to marketing your crafts online. If you come up with your own plan, by all means use it. The important point to remember is that the plan paints the picture of how you want your business to look when it's successful and keeps you from being distracted as you move around online.

Phase 1 - Keywords, search engines

Getting your Web pages to rank high in the search engines is listed first because search engine traffic is highly targetable and free. Therefore, you should take advantage of the free advertising right away.

• Define your Unique Selling Proposition -- in other words, what makes your product different. Whenever possible include your USP in your headline on your home page and printed promotional material.

• List 25 to 30 keywords and phrases people might use in searches to find your craft or Web site.

• Visit **WordTracker** and learn how many searches are done for each of your keywords. You will probably change the words you initially thought about and add to your list after doing research here.

• Optimize your pages by including those keywords in your META tags, image descriptions, comment tags and hyperlinks. Use WebPosition Gold software to automate search engine optimization.

• Register your Web pages at the top search engines by hand. Then consider registering at the minor engines using submission software.

• Register your site with *What's New* sites.

• If your budget allows, purchase your keywords at Overture.com.

• Schedule ongoing Web page updates and submissions of those pages to the major search engines.

• Check your rankings in the search engines every week because they might change. As needed, re-optimize your pages and resubmit.

Phase 2 - Links

• Search for your keywords on the major search engines. From the search results, make a list of all Web sites with subject matter like yours for seeking links and affiliate partners.

• Send emails to these sites' managers requesting links.

• Establish an ongoing schedule for continuing to seek links. Approach at least five sites a day.

• Use software like **Zeus** (described in the chapter on links) to automate the link seeking process.

• Track who has linked to your site by typing in "link:yourdomain.com" (without the quotation marks) at AltaVista.com, Hotbot.com or Google.com.

• After you have a list of who has linked to you, then check those sites the same way and see who has linked to them, providing you with more potential link partners.

Phase 3 - Email, newsletters, ezines

• Design your site to encourage visitors to register and provide you with their email address.

• Set up a database, online service and/or email manager program to store email addresses of customers, related Web sites, and affiliates.

• Create several different email signatures to attach to your outgoing emails. Each signature should include a link to a promotional message Web page.

• Consider investing in software to personalize emails for mass mailings or learn how to use word processing merge functions.

• Identify lists of opt-in email addresses for email promotions. Determine a budget for how much you will spend for renting opt-in lists.

• Set up autoresponders for providing canned replies -- answers to frequently asked questions.

• Create one or more newsletters or ezines around your craft subject matter.

• Set up a delivery system for your newsletter either with your own email manager or through a service like **groups.yahoo.com**.

• List your newsletter at all the online directories for ezines.

• Determine if you will sell classified ads in your newsletter. If so, create a Web page for ad rates.

• Collect opt-in contact information from your Web site visitors to receive information on related subjects. Earn money renting the email address list through brokers.

• Consider creating ecards from your craft product images to send to your email list. Link the ecard to your Web site. You can promote your ecards via all the methods described in this book.

Phase 4 - Newsgroups, forums, clubs

• Identify and list all newsgroups, forums and online clubs for subjects related to your crafts. Include AOL and Compuserve forums.

• Learn each group's rules for posting messages.

• Join as many groups as you can manage. Observe several posts before posting messages yourself. Only post helpful suggestions. Your email signature carries your promotional message.

• Send personal email to individuals who post questions answered by your craft. Give basic, helpful information and let your email signature point to your Web site.

• Create articles, free reports and give-aways that can be safely announced in newsgroups. Each article or report should carry a promotional tag.

• Post your site to announcement newsgroups.

• Start your own newsgroup. Or become an editor or moderator for an existing group or special interest site.

Phase 5 - Affiliate partners

• Determine if the selling price of your products allows for sharing revenues with affiliates. If so, establish a commission structure and pay-out terms.

• Set up a system for managing your affiliate program or use a service provider (recommended.)

• Create a Web page which describes your affiliate program. Include commission pay-outs, marketing materials they can use, and answers to frequently asked questions (FAQ's.)

• Double check your system to make sure everything functions properly.

• Use the list you created earlier of potential link partners to contact each site manager and announce your affiliate program.

• For additional income, include links to related products from other affiliate programs in your Web pages, emails, newsletters, and discussion group postings.

Phase 6 - Auction marketing

• Set up accounts with major auction sites.

• Create product images, text descriptions, 'more detailed product information' pages at your Web site, payment and shipping information.

• Place counters on your auction pages to track visitor numbers.

• Create several email replies that answer frequently asked questions. Save these in a file you can access and send quickly.

• Post your items for sale on auction sites.

• List your auction under many different category headings to attract more visitors.

• Set up zshop with Amazon.com.

• Use email to follow up with all bidders.

Phase 7 - Publicity

• Include your Web address on all printed materials, brochures, business cards, emails, catalogs, news releases and flyers.

• Write a news release about your product(s). Include contact information at the bottom.

• Write articles about your product(s). Most free article providers online will allow you to link to your Web site.

• Identify media appropriate to send announcements and articles to.

• When seeking TV appearances, create a sample script or list of questions the host can ask you.

Phase 8 - Advertising

• I recommend you use all the free methods of promotion outlined in this book first. However, the following list may be useful if you have the budget to test paid ads. Be sure to test a small population group before rolling out an offer to a larger, costlier audience.

• If budget allows, pay for relevant keywords at Overture.com.

• Write classified ads.

• Identify appropriate newsletters and ezines and place classified ads.

• Place classified ads on AOL and Compuserve.

• Identify Web sites appropriate to selling your craft through banner ads.

• Create several types of banner ads.

• Identify and join banner swapping programs.

• Create timetable for placing ads.

• Create tracking system to measure results from all ad campaigns.

• When your own Web site traffic reaches 10,000 or more visitors per month, decide if you want to sell advertising to other Web sites.

• Sell classified ads in your newsletter or ezine.

• Identify potential ad buying sites.

• Create ad rates page and agreement forms for your Web site.

• Identify and contact ad brokers to handle ad sales for you.

Phase 9 - Measure results

• Determine if and how much tracking your Web host provides.

• Determine if you want additional tracking service or software. Get page counters if needed.

• Set up a database or spreadsheet to store and sort tracking data. Track site visitors, ad results, link seeking results, search engine placements, email follow ups and all other promotions including offline marketing.

• Key all announcements, articles, ads and promotions so that you can measure response and sell-through rates for each.

• Use tracking on your Web pages to learn which pages get visited and which are ignored.

• Use your most visited pages to promote additional products.

• Create reports of your site traffic to show to prospective advertisers.

• Continually adjust promotional activities based on results.

Example of marketing activity schedule

Here's a sample list of daily action steps to take for promoting your books for one week.

Date	Action step
Monday	Seek links from 5 related Web sites
	Send news release to 2 online editors
	Write and send newsletter to house list
	Post 2 craft auction pages on Ebay.com auction site
Tuesday	Seek links from 5 related Web sites
	Post articles to 2 article sites
	Post comments to discussion group
	Post 2 craft auction pages on Ebay.com auction site
Wednesday	Seek links from 5 related Web sites
	Post 2 craft auction pages on Ebay.com auction site
Thurday	Seek links from 5 related Web sites
	Set up an online class to teach based on your craft
	Post 2 craft auction pages on Ebay.com auction site
Friday	Seek links from 5 related Web sites
	Post article for Valentine's Day tied to your craft
	Post 2 craft auction pages on Ebay.com auction site
	Measure results from previous month

Chapter 6 Success with Search Engines

Design your site to rank high in search engine queries. In other words, if you are making and selling fruit gift baskets and someone does a search for the keywords "fruit gift basket," you want your pages to show up at the top of the search results or at the very least on the first page of results.

Search engines are the most quoted way searchers find subjects they are looking for. How you rank will play a major role in how much traffic you get to your site, and consequently, how many sales you make.

In those searches for "fruit gift basket," if you show up on the first page of the search engine, you have a good chance of getting a visit. If you show up on the third page or later, forget it. The odds are against the seeker digging deeper. You can lose thousands of potential visitors and prospective sales.

Just listing your site with an engine is not enough. You have to know how search engines work in locating the seeker's query. Different search engines work in different ways, so it is important to look at each engine according to how it searches. Later in this chapter, resources are listed to help you keep up with each engine and how they change their criteria over time.

How search engines work

Search engines employ software called "spiders" to follow Internet hyperlinks that gather and record information about sites they visit. When you make changes to your site's pages, search engines find them and alter the way they rank you. Changes that affect your ranking include body text, page titles, meta tags, keywords and the number and quality of sites that link to you.

Spidering software checks for sites that you link to. The database behind the search engine is so huge that it contains records of all the links to all the sites it spiders. Popularity of a site is one of the key determinants of how your site is ranked. Therefore, your site may be ranked higher in the engines based on how many other sites have linked to you. Link seeking should be one of your top priorities. See the next chapter on how to get linked to.

It is important to post your individual pages frequently so that new links to you will add to a higher rank. However, never post the same page to a search engine more than once a day.

Each search engine works differently in how they filter the data they gather from your site. Some filter out your META tags, some include them.

If you build your site with frames, some engines will not read the text inside the frames without special html <NOFRAMES> tag. HotBot, Excite and Webcrawler do not read text in frames. One way around this problem is to build "doorway" pages (described later) without frames that the search engines can read but that lead the visitor to another page with frames. However, most good Web design theory recommends not using frames at all because of various problems including the inability of some older browsers to view pages with frames.

How search engines rank your site

Search engines rank your site based on many factors, some of the most important of which are centered around keyword usage:

- how many sites link to yours
- the quality of the sites that link to yours
- how keywords appear in your page title
- how often keywords appear in text on the page
- where in each paragraph keywords are found
- how keywords are included in link text
- how keywords are included in your domain name
- how keywords are included in the ALT tags for images
- how keywords appear in your META tags

Most of the major search engines have their own proprietary way of scoring relevancy and granting rank, which for the most part is secret. Search engines compete for getting more users and to become the most popular site to search from in order to earn money from advertisers.

The relevance scoring system for any engine will change from time to time. For this and other reasons, it is important to keep track of search engines and how they score for rank.

I use several resources that stay up to date on search engines. I consider these essential tools if you want to succeed at selling your crafts online. These programs and services get mentioned throughout this book. That's because they worked for me and many others. You will see results if you use these resources when promoting your site.

Top 10 tips to ranking high in the search engines

• Use the free service at **WordTracker** which gives you reports on how many times specific keywords are used in actual searches and tells you how many other web sites are competing with you for those words. Use this report to find appropriate keywords to include in your META tags and page design.

• Include your most important keywords in your domain name, headlines, page text, META tags, page titles, ALT text for images, and hypertext links.

• Use your keywords in folder names/subdirectories off your main site. This gives your site address more keywords for search engines to find.

• Place your keywords at the beginning and end of the text on your site and at the beginning and end of paragraphs. This is a higher scoring relevancy for many engines.

• Put your keywords together in phrases inserted in your Web page's text. Many people use more than one word in their search queries.

• Use your keywords frequently throughout your page text. To increase usage without making the reader wince, use different forms of the keywords. For instance, all of these words: crafting, crafted, handicraft, craftperson, and crafter contain the keyword craft and will count for relevancy by search engines.

• Post your Web pages by hand to the major engines and directories. Use software or a service company to post to the other engines.

• Avoid over using keywords to trick the search engines because they will just ignore your site altogether if they see too many keywords repeated.

• Use software to optimize your pages for highest ranking in the most important search engines. Keeping up with how the search engines rank sites can be a nightmare. I attempted to design and promote a site "by hand" alone. It was an impossibly complex and tedious task. Fortunately, I found Web Position Gold software that helps construct your pages for higher ranking, analyze competing sites, submit to the engines, track your results and updates itself regularly when the search engines change the way they rank keywords. Because of this software, many of my pages rank in the number one position at major engines like AltaVista, HotBot, MSN Search, Yahoo and others.

• Post each of your Web pages to each of the major engines daily, but no more than one page per engine per day. Most sites allow for regular postings. Every unique page gives you another way of attracting a niche audience.

• Get as many sites as you can to link to yours because this will boost your pages rankings. Use a free software program called Zeus to automatically locate all sites which would possibly link to yours. The more links to your site, the higher your ranking in the engines and directories. Get Zeus at **www.cyber-robotics.com**.

How directories work

Directories are listings based on descriptions you submit or reviews by the directory. The directory then searches your site to see if your description matches your site's contents. Changes you make on your site after listing do not affect your ranking so design your site for optimal ranking with the directories from the beginning.

If your site is content rich, well constructed and interesting, you are more likely to get reviewed by directories. Examples of directories are:

www.yahoo.com
www.google.com
www.bizweb.com
www.einet.net

Some search engines have accessory directories which may list your site if they like it enough to review it. Wherever you can find a "submit your site" or similar link, place your listing, even if there is no guarantee of getting an entry.

If your site is legitimate, that is, it isn't a front for a scam or adult site, you will probably get in most directories and engines with only a little effort. Yahoo! is the exception as it is estimated to only accept approximately one out of ten sites to be listed. In the appendix, you'll find more tips for listing at Yahoo.

For both Yahoo and LookSmart, one can pay a fee of around to get an express service review of your site - which means you will most likely get listed in the directory. Yahoo currently gets over half of all the Internet searches with LookSmart coming up a close second as LookSmart supplies listings to MSN Search and other engines. LookSmart claims they reach 77% of Internet users. If this is true, it's worth the price. See more details at **www.looksmart.com** and **www.yahoo.com**.

Paid listings that guarantee your Web pages are included in the Inktomi search index are available on a per Web page basis. Inktomi serves up results in major engines like AOL, MSN and Hotbot to name a few. The company that manages page listings for Inktomi is at **www.positiontech.com/inktomi/enroll.cfm** .

Search engines and directories people use most

Focus your major efforts on search engines and directories people use most to do their searching. The top engines listed in the list following are used by most people. The major engines are generally more reliable and kept up-to-date. Because these sites usually generate millions of dollars in advertising revenue, they are fiercely competitive for users.

This list of major search engines is listed according to approximate popularity derived from a survey of users. Search engine popularity differs from month to month. To keep current with changes in search engine usage, visit **www.searchenginewatch.com**.

When you go to the engine's home page, look for the "submit a site" or "add URL" link to take you their submission page. Post your pages to these top search engines and directories by hand or by using **Web Position** which keeps up to date with the search engine changes.

Yahoo - **www.yahoo.com** (go to the category you want to be listed under and follow the link to "add your URL.")

MSN - **www.msn.com**

Lycos - **www.lycos.com**

HotBot - **hotbot.lycos.com**

AltaVista - **www.altavista.com**

Google - **www.google.com**

Northern Light - **www.northernlight.com**

WebCrawler - **www.webcrawler.com**

Beyond the major engines there are hundreds of sites claiming to be search engines. Most of them however, will simply harvest your email address when you submit your site and then either send you SPAM or sell your email address to other SPAMMERS. Focus on the major engines where you will get most of your traffic from.

Next after the major engines, post your pages from these multi-posting sites:

the1000.com

www.gonetwide.com/gopublic.html

Additional legitimate engines to list your Web pages

www.2ask.com

www.alltheweb.com

www.buyersindex.com

www.comfind.com

www.directhit.com

www.dmoz.org

www.einet.net

handmade.net

www.infospace.com

www.nerdworld.com

www.infohiway.com

www.jayde.com

www.linkmonster.com

www.looksmart.com

peekaboo.net

www.scrubtheweb.com
www.searchalot.com
search.aol.com
search.thunderstone.com
www.usaol.com
www.where2go.com

Other sites to list with

www.canada.com   (Canadian search engine)

www.anzwers.com.au   (Australian search engine)

www.realnames.com   (Getting listed in the Real Names directory costs about $100.00 a year. It might be worth the price if you have a keyword phrase that is searched for often enough.) Visit their site and search for your keywords.

www.alco.com/. Look for the Free Index link. This page lists over 600 places to promote your site.

www.usatoday.com/life/cyber/ch.htm   USA Today has a hot sites editor reachable here.

Submitting your pages to search engines

When submitting to search engines, it helps to know that if you have a simple one or two page Web site, submitting the Web address alone — example: anysite.com — is sufficient to get all of your pages indexed. However, a site with many pages, like my craftmarketer.com requires that individual pages be submitted (one at a time) because the "spidering software" from the search engine may not probe deep into the site.

Submit a single Web page the same way you submit a domain Web address but the address is longer to include the individual page. For example, if I wanted to post a page about a free offer at the search engine's submission page, I would type in:

www.craftmarketer.com/working-woman-magazine.htm. If I were to only submit my domain name www.craftmarketer.com, some search engines might not "spider" the entire site to find other important pages that I want to show up in search queries.

Take time to submit each important web page separately, by hand. As mentioned, never submit more than one page from a single

Web site on the same day because the search engines interpret that as spam. There is no need to resubmit a page once submitted, unless you make changes to that page, in which case, definitely resubmit. Also resubmit your main URL if you make changes to a small Web site. However, you would not resubmit your pages to directories like: Yahoo.com, NBCi.com, dmoz.org. or About.com. Once you have been accepted and listed in the directories, you don't need to submit individual pages and doing so is a waste of time as they won't get re-indexed.

Be cautious using services or software which posts to hundreds of engines because, an out of date program can hurt your rankings more than help. The reason is that search engines change their submission page address and submission criteria. If you use a software program that is out of date, you don't get your pages posted or they get entered in the wrong manner. Use **Web Position** for submissions because it updates its guidelines automatically every few days.

There are only ten to twelve major engines and directories that most people use. To get traffic from high ranking pages, post your sites by hand to each of these engines.

There are free services that will submit your URL for you that are stay up to date. One good reason you might use these posting utilities is that as you get links from other sites, you can post that site's link page to the engines. This will not only increase your traffic from the link site, but boost your ranking with the engines. The more sites that link to yours, the higher your site is ranked. See **www.addme.com** and **www.gocee.com/eureka** .

Keywords

Keywords are what searchers look for. So it is crucial you construct your pages to include keywords used by searchers. If you use the wrong keywords, that is words or phrases your customers are not using, you lose. You have to learn to think like the searcher and you want to find out exactly what keywords or phrases searchers are using.

Before you begin submitting your pages to the search engines, make a list of your important keywords, site title and site description.

Create this list on paper or as a text file and keep it near your computer for quick reference. Use a word processor for easy cutting and pasting. You will be using this file frequently.

When a person types in a query (related words in question) at a search engine or directory, they get a list of sites or newsgroups where the query string can be found. Sites are listed in order of their relevance to the keywords according to the methods used by the search engine.

As an example, a weaver might logically come up with the following keywords to places on their site: "weaving, handwoven, hand made, woven by hand, handloomed"

Unfortunately, the weaver using these keywords listed might only attract other rug weavers looking for help with their own work. If one sells patterns and books on weaving, that's great. But if you are marketing your own products to sell, you won't get many qualified buyers.

A more effective strategy for keyword usage in the above example would be using words that describe products consumers search for like: "wearable art, scarf, women's clothing, fashion accessory, handmade gifts, handmade clothing, shawl, southwestern art." Once you know the actual keywords that get searched for, you can optimize your pages for ranking high on search engines. Although, you could learn to do this by hand, the process is painless and quick with **Web Position**.

For a craft person selling their work, choosing the right keywords is crucial. You don't want to only use keywords that describe your craft, you want to use keywords that potential buyers are actually using to find what they are looking for. Use the utility page at Overture.com described in the next couple of pages to learn exactly how many searches are done each month for a given word or phrase.

Doorway pages

One approach to increase your ranking in the search engines using keywords is to create "doorway" or "portal" pages to your site. These are pages specifically designed to rank high in the search engines based on their inclusion of keywords people are actually searching for like "gifts" or "wedding gifts" or "stocking stuffer."

The doorway page only exists to rank high in a query search. Once someone finds your page at a search engine and clicks on the link, they are taken to the doorway page. On that doorway page, you create links to your main site, but not back to the doorway page itself.

Since each search engine uses different criteria for selecting the ranking order of how pages appear in a search, to use the doorway page method successfully, you would want a separate doorway page for each engine and for each keyword. Rather than spend days and weeks researching search engine ranking methods, use **Web Position** software to create unlimited doorway pages for any number of keywords. One doorway page I created with this program reached the number one spot on a major search engine within six days of my submitting the page to the search engines.

For an example of a Web page optimized for ranking high on the MSN search engine with the keyword phrase "fashion accessory," see: **www.craftmarketer.com/fashion_accessory.htm**. The phrase "fashion accessory" appears at the beginning (but only once in each area) of these important page areas:
- page title - HTML title tag
- META keyword tag
- META description tag
- comment tag
- heading
- body text
- ALT tag for image
- hyperlink

I optimized this page for "fashion accessory" because when I ran a test for keyword usage at Overture.com described below, I discovered that approximately 1,500 to 2,000 searches are done each month across the Internet for the phrase "fashion accessory."

Over time, I plan to create more pages optimized for other keywords that draw potential customers like:
- "southwestern rugs" (600 to 700 searches)
- "wearable art" (1200 to 1500)
- "handmade gift" (800 to 1000)

One might think as I did at first that my logical choice keyword would have been "weaving" which is searched for four times as often as "fashion accessory," However, getting a high ranking for a page on "weaving" will most likely only bring me traffic from other weavers. I want buyers, not competitors, so I chose a phrase that prequalifies my traffic as those persons looking for something to wear.

A word of caution: if more than one of your doorway pages contains identical text, you may be penalized for attempting to SPAM. This is especially true at AltaVista. Therefore, vary each doorway page's content.

How do you know what keywords people are using?

Instead of guessing how people search, you can find out the actual terms used in queries. There are several sources that offer lists of which keywords people are using most:

• WordTracker.com provides a count of how many times keywords are included in searches. This is one of the most useful tools on the web! Enter a keyword or a phrase you are researching. WordTracker will give you a report on how many searches were done for that keyword and other related search terms that include the word(s).

This report helps you identify keywords to opimize your Web pages around -- exact keywords people are using in their searches every day. Here is a sample of search results in a 24 hour period from entering the keyword "gift basket" at WordTracker.

Count	Predicted	Keyword
466	2771	gift baskets
119	708	gift basket
22	131	gift basket supplies
21	125	holiday gift baskets
20	119	gift basket business
19	113	food gift baskets

Count	Predicted	Keyword
17	101	wine gift baskets
15	89	gift basket gourmet
13	77	baby gift baskets
11	65	gourmet gift baskets
11	65	fruit gift baskets
11	65	cookie gift baskets
9	54	gift basket ideas
9	54	making gift baskets

Numbers in the "Count" column are searches from the WordTracker database. Numbers in the "Predicted" column are the estimated total Internet searches. In the "Keywords" column is a list of related terms that people search for.

In the above example, over 2,700 Internet searches were estimated to have been done in a 24 hour period for "gift basket". Keep in mind that it's more useful to get qualified, prospective customer/visitors, as opposed to an increase in generic traffic. You will sell more products by ranking high for less-popular, but specific keyword phrases like "gourmet gift baskets" than attempting to be number one for more popular keywords like "gift baskets." The phrase "gourmet gift baskets" will pre-qualify potential customers for "gourmet gift baskets" you are selling.

WordTracker offers a free, but limited trial of their service that you can use as much as you want. The paid service offers analysis of how many other sites compete with your keywords and then gives you an estimate of what your chances are for getting a top ranking page. If you are at all serious about capturing the free traffic from search engines, this tool can put you way ahead of any competition.

Though not as specific as WordTracker, here are some additional tools for learning which keywords are being included in searches:

• **WordSpot** is a keyword search report site listing the top search requests for various keywords. The site offers three kinds of keyword reports depending on how much detail you want. Check these and any source lists you find at least once a month because the popular words change frequently. See **www.wordspot.com** .

• **Webcrawler** gives you a live broadcast of actual searches being done on their search engine at **www.webcrawler.com/voyeur_wc/**.

• **Lycos** lists the top 50 searches on their site at: **50.lycos.com/**
.

Pay-per-click search results

Overture.com leads the pack as far as pay-per-click search engines. Pay-per-click means that advertisers bid to be ranked higher for specific search terms. These advertisers pay sites like Overture.com for each visitor who clicks through from the search results to their Web sites.

For instance, three Web sites want their site to appear when a search is done for the keyword "craft patterns." One advertiser might bid five cents, another might bid eight cents and a third bidder might bid nine cents.

When someone searches for "craft patterns," the sites will appear in order of highest bid: the nine cent site appears first, then the eight cent site, then the five cent site. After the "paid for" results, appear unpaid results, from a generic search engine called Inktomi.

Be sure to test pay-per-click results to determine if buying traffic is cost effective. Remember that just because someone clicks through a search results link to get to your site, it doesn't mean they will buy your product.

Paying for results requires constant monitoring. For example, what if you bid ten cents and the nearest competing bid is only five cents. You are overpaying for traffic, because you only need to change your bid to three cents to get listed number one.

Additional pay-per-click search engines are listed and reviewed at: **www.payperclicksearchengines.com**

Measure your and your competitor's ranking in the engines

Wouldn't it be an advantage if you knew exactly where your site or anyone else with a site like yours is positioned in each of the major engines right now? One provider is Site Inspector - **www.siteowner.bcentral.com.** They can analyze your's or your competitor's site ranking in the major engines. Also, see **www.autosubmit.com/rateme.html**.

Web Position software gives you a "Reporter" function that will track how your pages rank on the major search engines by each keyword that you need to track.

TracerLock at **peacefire.org/tracerlock** can monitor search engines for you and notify you by email when a new instance of a search term is found. For example, if you tell TracerLock to monitor search engines for the word "handcarved" TracerLock will email you when new pages appear on the Web containing the word "handcarved."

Getting mentioned on What's New sites

Many Web surfers check out *What's New* or *What's Cool* sites. Imagine millions of visitors to your cool, new site! It takes some work to get reviewed by the owners as they look for truly unique new sites.

Before you get too excited about this avenue, remember that it isn't millions of general interest surfers you are looking for. You want visitors who are interested in your products enough to make a purchase.

Of course, if you sell some other service or product from your site, like those mentioned later in the chapter on associate programs, you will want any kind of extra traffic you can get.

Foreign search engines

Some search engines in other countries accept U.S. Web sites, others don't. And because policies change, you need to go to each engine to learn their current options. If you can produce a site in several languages, your chances of getting listed in an engine in those languages greatly improves.

To locate foreign search engines, start at **www.searchenginecolossus.com**.

Also, check **www.bizforms.com/search.htm.** The site's Foreign Language Search Engine Directory is categorized by country to help you register your Web site all over the WWW. Technically this directory is really a foreign country search engine listing, as English language search engines in foreign countries are included. The languages covered include Danish, Dutch, English, French, German, Italian, Japanese, Portuguese, Spanish and Swedish.

Researching the net

If you have conducted a simple search on one of several engines, you know that sometimes thousands or even millions of results can appear for some keywords. For those who are committed to learning Internet marketing, knowing how to conduct research is a required skill.

Fortunately, there are software tools to help you reduce the time needed to find sources of supplies, see sites like yours, and find sites that might link back to you. The following software programs conduct multi-search engine queries and deliver all results in a catalog format allowing you to complete research tasks in a relatively short time. These tools are more efficient than multiple search engine sites because they find listings not included by the other engines. I like Copernic and Bulls Eye because they are both free.

Copernic - **www.copernic.com** (free)

BullsEye - **www.IntelliSeek.com** (free)

Mata Hari - **thewebtools.com** (free trial)

In addition to these search programs, there are multiple search engine sites online. Depending on your tasks at hand, these sites below might give you slightly faster results than the above mentioned softwares. However, you will probably get more finely tuned results when using Copernic or BullsEye.

Sites which search multiple engines:

SavvySearch - **www.savvysearch.com** - You select from scores of engines or other sites to search and integrates the results.

All-in-One Search - **www.allonesearch.com** - posts fields for searching more than 400 engines, directories, and specialized sites. It searches each engine separately.

Ask Jeeves - **www.askjeeves.com** - allows natural-language queries like phrases.

DeBriefing - **www.debriefing.com** - digs up links using seven engines/sites, deletes duplicates, and even offers keywords to narrow your search.

Dogpile - **www.dogpile.com** - conducts Web metasearches using 13 different engines/directories and Usenet, but it doesn't eliminate duplicates.

Go2net - **www.go2net.com** - queries other search engines, then scores the findings for each search.

Mamma - **www.mamma.com** - searches seven sites.

Keeping current with search engine technology

The ways in which search engines and directories do searches changes as technology advances. To keep abreast of these changes and how they will affect your Internet business, check out these resources:

Newsgroups:

alt.internet.search

alt.internet.search-engines

comp.infosystems.search

Newsletters:

www.researchbuzz.com/news -- newsletter covering the search tools and online research. Lots of information. Free subscription. Weekly news.

www.searchengineguide.com -- Search Engine Guide is a free newsletter on search engines. Arrives daily.

Software:

www.craftmarketer.com/web-position-software.htm -- The best of software solutions is WebPosition. I mention this software many times throughout this book for one significant reason - it works! I would not even attempt to market my Web sites without it. It allows you to analyze, track, and monitor multiple domain names with an unlimited number of keywords and phrases. **WebPosition**

creates summary reports as well as detail reports that show you all the sites that are above and below you in the rankings. WebPosition checks your site's visibility in major search engines, including: AltaVista, Excite, HotBot, LinkStar, Yahoo!, WebCrawler, InfoSeek, Lycos, Magellan, Northern Lights, WWW, and YellowPages. Most of my pages created and submitted by Web Position rank in the top ten results of searches - several are at the number one position in the major engines.

www.positionagent.com -- WebPosition Agent is a subscription service that automatically tracks where your site is in 10 top search engines and directories. You pay for 6 months of service, and submit URL/keyword pairs for the service to monitor. Using your keywords, PositionAgent generates reports showing where your site's pages rank within each of the search engines. PositionAgent has a free trial at positionagent.linkexchange.com/free.htm. The trial version is limited to a single URL/keyword pair and is somewhat more limited in its reports than the full version, but still yields useful data about your Web site's position in the top search engines.

Chapter 7 How to Use Links to Boost Traffic

Recent surveys showed that next to search engines, following a link was the second most common way visitors found sites. Getting a site with similar subject matter and high traffic to link to your site is one of the best means of getting qualified traffic.

The more quality sites that link to you, the higher your popularity and the better your ranking will be among the search engines. It makes sense then to strive to get as many links to your site as possible, preferably from sites with good content and high traffic.

You may ask why would a competing site link to you? Direct competitors may not, but there are enough sites that will link to you to make the pursuit worthwhile. Remember that the Internet was created as a means of sharing information, mostly for free. Although we are certainly commercializing the web, there will continue to be a large audience searching for free material. Sites that provide links to information or content of interest will get traffic.

One of my Web sites was recently completed and ready for posting in the search engines. Since most of the engines take weeks and sometimes months to spider a site, I began a planned approach for seeking links from craft related sites. Within a week of starting to seek links, and subsequently receiving several, I began logging over 80 to 100 unique visitors a day from link traffic alone.

Getting other sites to link to yours

Identify and list sites whose subject matter complements your site's content. To do this, search for your keywords and keyword phrases at the major search engines. Make a list of the sites that come up. You can also use reverse searching techniques mentioned later in this chapter or the software program called Zeus described later here.

Visit each related site and go through several of their pages. Look for the address of the webmaster or site owner. Send a personal email to them explaining why you think their visitors would benefit from learning about your site. Complement the owner on his or her site, but don't blindly flatter. If you really looked through their site, you can point out a feature that caught your eye. Keep the note personal and brief. Ask for a link and offer to reciprocate. Include your URL so they can review your site.

For example, your site may provide a free article on making wooden gift boxes. After visiting a woodworking site with other articles on the subject, you approach the webmaster mentioning that visitors who read their article might also enjoy reading yours. Include the URL for the webmaster to see the article. If your site provides free information that complements another site, the other site may feel they gain added credibility by linking to you.

Send an email asking the webmaster to look at your site and exchange links. However, be sure to personalize your email as much as possible. A mass mailing to many webmasters will most likely be interpreted as SPAM which will only damage your credibility.

Don't just ask any site for a link exchange. Target sites whose visitors would likely visit you, especially those with high traffic.

When seeking links to my site from the top ranking sites in the search engines, I found most webmasters friendly and quite willing to exchange links.

Make sure to follow up a week or two later to see that the promised link appears on the other site. If you don't find the link to your site, send a very brief note something like this:

Dear Bob,
*   I wanted to let you know I have place your link on our site's link pages along with a brief description. Please check it out at*
www------.
Regards,
Jim

This kind of note will remind them of your previous agreement to exchange links without appearing pushy.

Even after you have gotten several links to your site, continue the activity of seeking links from related sites. Make this activity an ongoing priority. New sites will appear every month and links to you are a terrific means of raising your traffic.

Automating the link seeking process

Software exists to automate the tasks of seeking relative sites, gathering the email addresses of the owners, ranking the relevance of the site to your keywords and sending email requests to these sites requesting a link exchange. In addition, the software builds a "Link Directory" on your site which is organized by subject. Though there are several programs that accomplish tasks like these, the one I like best is free software called *Zeus*. You can download the free software at **www.cyber-robotics.com.**

Link banner exchanges

Link banner exchange programs are another way of promoting through getting link traffic. Unfortunately, some people use software that filters banners from their browser screen.

Still, you will get visitors from banners if your banner content is highly targeted. And it doesn't cost you anything but a small amount of time to get involved in a link exchange program. Banner exchanges can get free traffic to you before the search engines have spidered and ranked your pages.

To make banner exchange programs worthwhile, you want to identify programs with high traffic sites that have subject matter complementary to yours.

Below is a list of the more popular link exchange programs. Their trade ratios vary and may even change from the time of this printing so visit each site to see what each program offers.

A word of caution: read any link exchange program's agreement thoroughly. Check each program to make certain they don't allow "adult" site material. The last thing you want is a porno banner showing up on your craft site.

www.1for1.com
www.adbility.com
www.bannerswap.com

www.businessnation.com
www.hitexchange.net
www.impressionz.com
iwr.com/free/links.htm
www.linkexchange.com
www.linkbuddies.com
www.momsnetwork.com

Where to place banners on your pages

Where banner ads are placed on your page affects the number of click-throughs that banner receives. Studies show that banner ads at the bottom of Web pages pull higher response rates. Not only will you get a higher click through rate on banners at the bottom of pages, folks will take in your entire page before clicking away to another site.

How to get banners

If you don't have a graphics program for generating banners, there are many free resources on the web. Many of the banner exchange programs mentioned earlier offer free banner creation tools:

www.animationonline.com
www.coder.com/creations/banner
www.crecon.com/banners.html
www.ezart.com
www.goodwebs.com
www.mediabuilder.com
members.tripod.com/~flinda/index.html
quickbanner.com/index.dbm?system=havenhood
www.web-animator.com
www.zyweb.zy.com

How to verify your links

Over time, links you added from your site to other Web sites or to pages within your own site may need verifying. If you are working with a software for generating pages that does not provide tools for link verification, there is a free program called Xenu. Xenu is capable of checking Web sites links as large as thousands of pages and very quickly. Get a free copy of Xenu at

www.snafu.de/~tilman/xenulink.html

The Web sites below will check links for free as a trial of their link checking software. You can find other software by searching for "HTML link checker" at the search engines.

www.coast.com
www.elsop.com/linkscan/quickcheck.html
www.incontext.com
www.linkalarm.com
www.netmechanic.com
www.SEVENtwentyfour.com
degraaff.org/checkbot
websitegarage.netscape.com

Measuring your site's popularity with reverse searching

Reverse searching tells you who is linking to your site. Some search engines like AltaVista, Infoseek and HotBot allow "reverse or backward searching." This is accomplished through "field searching" within the search engine's database which means you are focusing your search on the field in the database called "link."

To do a reverse search through a search engine, enter your (or any other) Web page address in the search box and preface the address with "link:" and without the "www" preceding your site name.

Here's an example: "link:craftmarketer.com." At HotBot, you would enter "linkdomain:craftmarketer.com" and find out which sites had links to the craftmarketer.com site.

A handy site that will do reverse searching for you at three major search engines is **www.wsabstract.com**. For another quick free reverse search, see **www.linkpopularity.com**.

There are more ways to make use of reverse searching. Say that you have done a search for your keyword, "stained glass" and your site comes up four pages down into the search. You want to improve your ranking because few people take the time to go past the first page of their search.

Since one of the ways you can advance your ranking is to increase the number of quality sites that link to you, you can use reverse searching to find out who is linking to those top ranking sites that come up in keyword searches for "stained glass." Now you have a list of new possible sites to create relationships with - sites that were unknown to you before the reverse search.

Sites for craft artists to seek links from

Seek links from other sites on a daily basis to increase your popularity ranking in the search engines and thus, increase your positioning when someone does a search for your keywords. Here's a list of sites to start with that will link to arts and crafts related sites:

www.artcents.com/artguide/add.html
www.artcrawl.com
www.artmarketing.com
www.artsearch.net/urlform.html
art.net/Links/linksform.html
www.artpromote.com
www.auntie.com
www.bestwayimaging.com/catalog/linkss.html
www.bobbilynn.com/addlinksform.html
www.buyersindex.com
www.catalog.com/giftshop/icd/icd1.htm
www.chebucto.ns.ca/~aj514/crafts.html
crafterscatalogs.com
crafterscommunity.com
www.crafters-market.com
crafters.net/cgi/topvlog.cgi?937847230
www.craftsfaironline.com
www.craftmarketer.com
craftylinks.com
www.doubletakeart.com
www.eastplaza.com/crafts/forms/ad_a_link.htm
www.msn.fullfeed.com/~wrldcrft/links.html
www.handilinks.com/index.php3
www.innerart.com/addlink.html
www.myfree.com

www.netcrafts.com/index.sht
www.reciprocallink.com/directory
www.supermall-association.com/template/
FreeSubmitForm.cfm
www.thecountrygallery.net/index.htm
www.totalseek.com
www.wood-n-crafts.com
worldartistdirectory.com
www.wwar.com
www.wwwresources.com/free/ffal/ffa.cgi?id=2-208
www.wyomingcompanion.com/janacraft/links2.htm

A site that will help you identify additional craft sites appropriate for exchanging links is at:

www.reciprocallink.com/directory

Chapter 8 Promoting Through Email and Ezines

Email is a free way of keeping in touch with existing customers and converting new prospects into paying customers. Email is considered by many to be the best of all marketing tools because it doesn't cost you anything, it goes anywhere around the globe, anytime 24 hours a day, 365 days a year and email allows you to build relationships with your customers.

People will visit your site if you have done your job in getting their attention. Once they get to your site, you want ways to capture their names and email addresses.

How much is this contact information worth to you? If you have kept a mailing list of customers who buy from you through other means such as craft fairs, you already know what percentage of customers are likely to buy from you again if you mail them an offer. If you haven't been accumulating customer contact information, start right away. Your own mailing list is like a gold mine you continue to get returns from for many years.

This chapter is about ways to get your visitors to leave you their email contact information, how to locate other lists of names of prospective customers, and how to use these emails to increase your sales.

What not to do: bulk email, SPAM, unsolicited email

Nobody likes SPAM or unsolicited email. SPAMMING is transmitting massive amounts of email to big lists of general email addresses. Advertisers use this method like bulk mail that arrives in your regular mail box. There are movements underway to make bulk email or SPAM illegal. California has a law against it and other states are considering similar legislation.

There are several ways that bulk mailers get email addresses. Frequently they employ software to locate and spider newsgroup postings. The software searches on specific keywords present in the postings like "dogs" or "vegetarian cooking." Then, the software harvests the emails out of those messages accumulating hundreds, even thousands of names per hour. The rental rates vary for these names, but I've been offered 10 million names for about $200.

In many cases, you can acquire emails of newsgroup members yourself by joining the group. Many newsgroups allow access to the list of members. If the newsgroup does not allow access to members, you can go through the archives and collect members' emails from the postings. If you follow this method, be sure to approach any kind of mailings of names of people who have not yet visited your site with great care. Personalized email to these newsgroup members might get you some new names if your message isn't deemed as SPAM.

I highly recommend you do not SPAM through email. There are practical reasons for this:

• Your ISP will shut you down at the first few complaints - and there will be complaints. Some people may sue you, harass you, or subscribe you to all kinds of unwanted newsletters.

• You have to spend time and money finding another provider.

• People disrespect your company name. For the artist trying to build a name, bulk emailing is a serious public relations blunder.

I read a description of a SPAMMER as being like someone on a street corner who kicks passersby in the shins and then hands them an advertising flyer.

Your house mailing list

Your first and best source of emails will be names you garner from your Web site. This list is often referred to as your house list. Your house list names will usually generate the highest response to any promotions where your name or company name is recognizable to recipients. If you rent a list that proves to have a better response rate than your house list, get those names into your database.

Visitors to your site are most likely not to be offended if you mail announcements or product news via email. They certainly won't mind receiving your emails if they have been asked ahead of time for their permission to get such news.

Opt-in email lists

In addition to your own list of names, you may want to build your customer base by reaching out to new prospective buyers who have made it known they wish to receive announcements for products or services like yours. These email lists are known as opt-in lists or permission lists.

Verify that any company promising you opt-in names is providing emails of persons who specifically request to receive related subject material. I have received several unsolicited email ads from persons claiming to have opt-in lists for sale. However, since I got their offer through SPAM, it is safe to assume the emails they are offering for sale are also unsuspecting victims. For your own protection, email only to those who have specifically requested to receive your information or material on specific subjects.

Sources for reputable opt-in mail lists include:

www.liszt.com/directmail.html

www.postmasterdirect.com

www.targ-it.com

e-target.com/?webthemes

www.yesmail.com

How to get email addresses from your visitors

There are several ways to capture your visitors' email. But in every instance, all you really have to do is get them to click on a button.

Give something away - Including a link that reads like this: Click here to receive a free sample will most likely get a high number of click throughs. Another effective enticement is to offer free information. Free information is what most people are searching the Web for.

Subscribe to a newsletter/mailing list - This is a fantastic method, because when they click, it means they're specifically asking you to contact them. They're saying to you *"I don't want to buy anything right now, but I want to keep in touch with you in case you have something to offer in the future"*.

Join your discussion group - Run a discussion group on a subject that your product or service relates to. You can promote your own product freely, although you will want to be subtle in order to keep your readers coming back. You'll capture the emails of your subscribers. A note of warning if you intend to run a discussion group, you'll have to monitor the incoming messages frequently to prevent unwanted ads or undesirable material from appearing.

Take part in a survey - Suppose you conduct a survey about an important or controversial event. You could create a form that logs visitors email and their comments. This method of getting emails will take time and effort because you have to let everyone know later the results of the survey.

Offer a free report - Use the autoresponder method described later in this chapter.

Offer a coupon as an incentive - Coupons are used by approximately 88% of the online population. See the programs below. You can require a registration form to be filled in to receive the coupon. The registration form can require email and physical address information.

Have a contest - See the section on contests in Chapter 4 on making your site interactive.

If you need help in producing forms that process visitors' input, check out the free scripts for creating a wide variety of forms at **www.worldwidemart.com/scripts/**. Many Web authoring software programs like FrontPage2000 include "wizards" that produce forms for your specifications.

Using Internet incentive programs

While you certainly can develop your own online incentive programs to entice visitors to leave you their emails, it may be easier to use a provider. Incentive or loyalty programs have existed offline for decades in forms like *Green Stamps* and *Frequent Flyer* miles.

Many of the programs listed here offer the ability to print coupons from your computer or to gather points for visiting sponsoring sites. Points can then be exchanged for products and services. Some programs allow affiliate or associate members to offer the incentives to their customers.

www.coolsavings.com
www.cybergold.com

www.e-centives.com
www.freeride.com
www.mypoints.com
www.webstakes.com
www.ebates.com

How to promote with direct email

You can use direct email to market your products much the same way as doing a postal mailing, without the expense of printing, postage and labor. In a direct mail campaign, you must test different offers before rolling out to a large list. Suppose you are looking into renting a list of 30,000 opt-in names of persons interested in gift baskets. A good way to start would be to mail four different offers to a sampling of 100 names each. The offer that pulls the best response would then be rolled out to a larger group from the list, like 1,000 names. If you get similar results to the smaller mailing, you know the list is good and you can mail to the remaining names as your budget allows.

For craftpersons who sell their work, the basic direct email campaign might contain a brief letter announcing a new product or a special closeout on items you are discontinuing. In your email, you can mention a Web page address that gives more details. Keep your email announcements brief because most people will not read long emails.

Rather than send out one email to a list of names, you will get a higher response rate - as much as double - by personalizing the email offer. If you have a large email list, it would be too time consuming to do this by hand. WorldMerge software automatically personalizes your message to your list of targeted customers.

You will want a contact list of all the names, emails, and postal addresses of your customers and prospects. Using an email manager program like those mentioned below, you can send your promotional messages to large groups of emails that meet criteria you set up.

For instance, you mail an announcement offering a 50% off special on earrings you want to discontinue. Your first message goes out to your entire list of say, 750 emails. After one week, you go through your sales orders making a list of all those who bought from the email list.

Let's say you sold to 30 customers. Create a second email group with the original 750 emails minus the 30 who bought. Now you are ready to send out another follow-up message to those who did not buy the first time. You could continue this program as long as you are getting some percentage of response that makes the activity worth your time. Remember, you aren't paying anything to send out the emails.

It is fairly well known in mail order that it takes at least seven contacts to a prospect before they buy. If you are consistent with your online contacts your name or craft will become familiar to your prospects. The more people recognize your name and craft, the more apt they are to trust you. People buy from those they trust.

Managing your list

As mentioned before, I use and recommend **Pegasus**, a free email manager. **Eudora Pro** is another excellent program. Both of these email managers are capable of creating and managing large lists - sometimes referred to as distribution lists - to whom you can mail out one message.

Another great way to use an email manager is for emailing a newsletter or ezine to your customer base of emails. Each month, you write the newsletter and then email it to the entire list. Within minutes everyone gets your email. Use the "distribution list" or "group" function in your email program because when the message is sent to a group, the recipients don't see the other recipients' names. All the emails that have gone bad since you last updated your list will be returned to you as undeliverable, which you can then delete from your email address book.

There are other more sophisticated (and more costly) email programs to help you manage direct mail campaigns. One program called PostMaster runs around $300. PostMaster automates the tasks of managing your database list with scheduled email letters to lists you designate. Get a free trial of the software at
www.post-master.net

How to get and use autoresponders

Autoresponders are pre-written emails from you which are sent automatically to a person who clicks on an email link to the preconfigured autoresponder. Autoresponders are capable of sending the same message to thousands of people within moments. On your part, you never have to lift a finger once the autoresponders are set up.

After viewing your Web page or classified ad or email message, a viewer chooses to get additional information from you by hitting a 'click-to' button or link. When they click, they are emailing an (invisible) request to the address of your autoresponder which automatically sends them your report or additional information which somewhere contains your promotional message.

At the same time, your autoresponder can send a carbon copy of the message to your own designated email address when you set it up to do so. This will give you the email address of the person placing the request. You will want to add all these new email addresses to your database.

Track your marketing efforts by simply instructing the requestor to enter a specific message in the subject area. For instance, you place classified ads with an autoresponder email address for a free report. If you want to learn which ads pull the best, have each ad give a different instruction for what goes into the subject line. In one ad, you instruct the reader to place 'History of Weaving - Free Report' in the subject line. In another ad, you tell them to write in 'Weaving History Report.' Now you have two different "keys" to measure responses to determine which ad sources you want to keep and which ones to drop or make changes to.

You can purchase autoresponders, or increasingly more often, you can find them free or included with Web hosting services. To locate providers, do a search at any major search engine for "autoresponders".

One of the ways I market my products is by creating free reports which are delivered by autoresponder. Once the autoresponder is set up, I never have to touch the email again unless I want to update the information.

After creating the article inside an autoresponder email, I post the address of the autoresponder email on classified ad sites all over the net. To locate these sites, do a search on any engine for the phrase "free classified ads."

Here is an example of how an autoresponder works. Send a blank email to **pricing@craftmarketer.com** and within seconds, you receive a free report on pricing your craftwork. At the end of the report is instructions on how to order *The Basic Guide to Pricing Your Craftwork* from which the report is taken. You can do the same for craft items, patterns, tools, prints and posters and anything else you sell.

Ways to use autoresponders to increase traffic and sales:

• Post messages in newsgroups on your subject with the offer of a free informative article that you offer via autoresponder.

• Work with related Web site owners by requesting they link to your autoresponder's address which sends a free article - written to inform and lead to a sale - to their existing visitors.

• Look for related Web site owners who do not currently use autoresponders as follow-ups or confirmation of orders. Offer to provide them the autoresponder at no charge as long as you can mention your free article via another autoresponder and mention your URL. Sites with large traffic could be persuaded by offering to pay them a percentage of resulting sales.

• Post classified ads which get responses to your autoresponder for a free article.

Setting up the autoresponders are usually quite simple and instructions come with them.

Send out a free email newsletter or ezine

An ezine or electronic magazine is a free newsletter sent out to a targeted group of readers who have chosen to subscribe because of their interest in the subject matter. The most effective ezines are those that focus on delivering real content to their readers. Some advertising is often found in ezines, but the more effective publications keep ad content to a minimum.

One function of an ezine is to keep in regular touch with prospects and customers. Create customer loyalty by educating and entertaining readers, not by hard selling them. The more often you contact your list, the more likely they will remember you. Most importantly, subscribers have specifically requested to be on the list to receive the newsletter. This is not SPAM, where readers get unsolicited bulk email from advertisers.

Offering a free newsletter is another method of generate more traffic to your Web site. Create a sign-up page for the newsletter on your site and promote it to all the search engines. Everyone loves freebies.

To get a feel for what you want yours to look like, subscribe to several ezines through some of the list directories that follow. Most of the layout has to be simple because email does not allow for the kind of fancy page styles that you can put up on Web sites.

For a small list of from a few hundred to 1,000 emails that you mail messages to you can easily use Pegasus or EudoraPro. For larger lists, the tasks of keeping up with subscribers and unsubscribers is best automated. For tools and news about creating and managing ezines and mailing lists, here are some resources to help:

www.e-zinez.com
www.list-business.com
www.listbot.com
www.list-city.com

Sources of ezine listings

In addition to promoting your ezine through search engines, you can list your newsletter at the large list directories.

Places to list your ezine:

aae.freeservers.com/listings.html
www.egroups.com
www.ezineseek.com
www.ideamarketers.com
www.liszt.com (over 90,000 lists)
www.neosoft.com/internet/paml
www.netmastersolutions.com
www.oblivion.net/zineworld
www.wilsonweb.com/webmarket/ezines.htm

Here's two newsletters that are just for announcing new newsletters:

www.egroups.com/subscribe/aannounce
www.egroups.com/subscribe/ezine_announce

Make money renting your email list

If you build a large mail list through your site and want to earn extra income through renting those names to others, engage a mail list broker who specializes in renting opt-in email lists. You can find them by going through the directories of ezine listings already listed. Here are two more sites that will help:

www.list-city.com
www.liszt.com/directmail.html

Understand that your customers probably will not appreciate your renting their name unless they specifically ask to receive advertising information on a given subject.

Ecards

A phenomena that has made great gains in popularity on the Internet is electronic gift cards or ecards, sent as email attachments. Just to give you an idea of how huge this market has become, one of the innovators in this arena, **BlueMountain.com**, a provider of free ecards was at one time the 6th most visited site online.

One way artists are utilizing this way of marketing is to hook up with an existing ecard company. The ecard company probably won't pay you for your designs but will provide a link somewhere on the ecard that takes the viewer to your site.

Because of the tremendous growth in this field, there are too many electronic card sites to mention here. Do a search for "electronic cards" at **www.dogpile.com** and you will have your hands full for some time. One site with environmental values that provides reciprocal link arrangements for artists is:

www.care2.com/help/ecards/art.html

One of the most effective use of ecards in your marketing is to create electronic cards as follow ups to your customers. What could be a better way of putting images of your work in front of your customers several times a year around holidays and special occasions?

How to use signatures in your emails

A signature is a message footer attached to the bottom of your email. Most email managing software allows you to create from one to several different signatures and then gives you an option to choose to add a signature when sending your emails. If your program does not allow signatures, find and use one that does, like Pegasus or Eudora.

As you post responses to emails or newsgroups, use a signature which briefly entices readers to your site or an autoresponder message. Include a signature on all your email messages. This takes advantage of the possibility that those receiving your email might forward your message to friends.

Signatures should only be a few lines at the most. Create several, each of which includes a specific marketing message. It has been found effective to include a URL in your signature to which recipients can click on and go straight to your Web page. Example of an email signature:

> **=-=--Visit James' Catalog of Handmade Ornaments =-==-**
> =-=-=-= at < www.handmadeornaments.com > =-=-=-=-
> =-James' Ebay <members.ebay.com/aboutme/james/>-=

Note that there are two URL's in the above signature. One points the viewer to the Web site catalog and the second address takes the viewer to a descriptive page at an auction site on ebay.com. See Chapter 11 How to Use Online Auctions for Selling Crafts.

8 ways to use email to boost sales

• Use email to follow up with customers and site visitors thanking them for their interest in your work. Take advantage of the follow up to mention a future event which you will be attending in their area to show your newest pieces. Consider making a special offer or incentive to get visitors to return to your site.

• Rent opt-in email lists for direct email campaigns.

• Create an electronic newsletter or ezine.

• Run a discussion group.

• Send electronic cards with images of your craft work. Ecards will be especially effective around holidays, birthdays and special occasions. Encourage your recipients to pass on the ecard to their friends who might visit your site.

• Write useful, interesting articles which can be retrieved though email autoresponders. Within the article, include a link to a Web page with your promotional message. Place your autoresponder emails in all your promotions.

• Every email you send should include a signature at the end which leads the visitor to a promotional Web page or an autoresponder message.

• Rent your email list of visitors and customers to email list brokers. Of course, make sure you have your email owners' permission to receive offers of interest similar to what's at your site.

Chapter 9 How to Promote on Newsgroups, Forums and Discussion Lists

Newsgroups and discussion lists came about as a way for readers to get and give help on specific topics. Get others to notice your craft site through participating in newsgroups and forums where people post messages about a specific subject of interest.

Similar to newsgroups, are Internet mailing lists. The difference is that newsgroups and forums are accessible by the public while mailing lists are delivered via email. One of the largest list directories is at **www.liszt.com** which lists over 90,000 Internet mailing lists. Newsgroup topics cover anything from craft patterns to art history to selling on the Internet.

By following the rules which we'll talk about in this chapter, you can successfully promote your crafts on the public newsgroups or through a forum which you organize and maintain. Rules of etiquette for posting to newsgroups are stringent, however, and if you attempt to SPAM a group in any way, you will do more harm than good to your business. The reasons for not using SPAM email to promote your product are true for newsgroups. Violate this "netiquette" and you will get flamed or worse, your host may shut you down.

Whether you are monitoring your own newsgroup or a public list, as you watch new messages day to day, you will find many opportunities to answer individuals directly. You can build a relationship with individuals by answering their questions as an expert in your field. In many cases, you won't have to be blatant about your promotion because your email signature carries your marketing message.

Posting on forums and newsgroups will create business for you down the road because once people know and trust you, they are more likely to buy from you. However, the process takes time so be aware you need to cultivate this method of marketing before it bears fruit.

If you are not prepared to contribute something to others in the group in a meaningful way, newsgroups are not an avenue you should pursue. And in the long run, there are many other means of promoting your site that take less time and bring faster results. Still, if you have extra time, this method can help you build your business.

Prepare an announcement

You may not be able to advertise your craft on newsgroups but you can place an announcement if written correctly. An example of an appropriate announcement to a newsgroup for doll enthusiasts is:

> Would you like to receive an article on the history of doll making? If so, please send an email to me with a subject line of "Send doll making." I'll send you the article, "History of Doll Making" by me, Dana Dolls, author and creator of many popular doll patterns. The article is a fascinating account of the first dolls and how doll making has been done throughout the centuries. You'll probably learn some great tips for making your own dolls. You can get this article at my Web site: www.danadolls.com.

An inappropriate post to the doll group would be an announcement for a business opportunity program you are promoting.

The best way to tell whether your announcement is acceptable is to spend some time studying recent postings to a newsgroup you are targeting. In the other postings, did advertisers get flamed? What sort of announcements didn't get flamed? Does the group have an FAQ page and rules for posting.

Also, take note of what others type in the subject line of their postings. Some readers may not even open postings with commercial sounding subject text.

The more focused the subject of your newsgroup, the easier it will be to know what you can type into the subject line of your posts. Although this may seem obvious, doll makers will be interested in articles about doll making.

The most effective offers are those giving something away for free. Contests are good, too. Whatever you post, keep it brief - one or two paragraphs - but no more than can be viewed in one screen.

Somewhere in the text of your announcement you lead your reader to a Web page or an autoresponder with a longer message. In traditional mail order marketing, this is called the two-step approach. Likewise on the Internet, the first step is to get them to do something easy like click on a link. In the second step you present your offer.

Posting your message

Posting to a newsgroup is simple. Most browsers have a news reader built in. The news reader goes out to Usenet and pulls in the messages from the newsgroups you subscribe to. The news reader also allows you to subscribe and unsubscribe from the lists.

Post your message to each group by hand. If you attempt to post the same message to multiple groups, you can run into problems and take the risk of your message being viewed as SPAM.

Types of newsgroups

There are many kinds of discussion lists you can post announcements to. Groups fall into two categories, moderated and unmoderated. If the group is unmoderated, postings will be full of ads. Moderators control material posted to moderated groups.

Types of newsgroups:

Newsgroups on Usenet

AOL forums and discussion groups

CompuServe forums and discussion groups

Internet mailing lists

Newsgroups and forums for crafts

Whatever your art or craft, there are many newsgroups about that topic. The newsgroups listed below are for craft related topics. The groups shown here may be more valuable to you as networking opportunities than for promotion purposes. However, if you sell supplies or services to other crafters, these lists will bring you in touch with a wealth of contacts. See the chapter on affiliate marketing for ideas on other programs to offer your visitors.

You may or may not be able to access these list through your current browser because different newsgroups are available through different channels. If you have a problem finding a newsgroup on your browser, go to one of the major search engines like **yahoo.com** and do a search for the newsgroup by name and then follow the link(s).

alt.binaries.pictures.crafts
alt.crafts.blacksmithing
alt.crafts.candlemaking.soapmaking.moderated
alt.crafts.plastic-canvas
alt.crafts.print-artist
alt.crafts.professional
alt.rec.crafts.metalworking
alt.sewing
net.crafts.general
net.crafts.general.marketplace.commercial
net.crafts.metalworking.general
net.crafts.textiles.general
net.crafts.textiles.marketplace.commercial
net.crafts.woodworking.general
pei.crafts
rec.crafts.
rec.crafts.beads
rec.crafts.carving
rec.crafts.dollhouses
rec.crafts.glass
rec.crafts.jewelry
rec.crafts.marketplace
rec.crafts.metalworking
rec.crafts.newsgroup
rec.crafts.misc
rec.crafts.polymer-clay
rec.crafts.pottery
rec.crafts.quilting
rec.crafts.rubberstamps

rec.crafts.textiles.machine-knit
rec.crafts.textiles.marketplace
rec.crafts.textiles.misc
rec.crafts.textiles.needlework
rec.crafts.textiles.quilting
rec.crafts.textiles.sewing
rec.crafts.textiles.yarn
rec.crafts.woodturning
rec.woodworking

Locating more newsgroups and forums

You can search for a wide range of newsgroups by:

• Using Internet Explorer and Netscape Navigator because they allow you to access newsgroups through a menu in the browser.

• Exploring Deja News at **dejanews.com** for a good source of newsgroups. At the site, search for: comp.infosystems.www.announce

• Doing a subject search at one of these directories:

www.listtool.com
paml.net
www.newsville.com
tile.net/lists
www.forumone.com
www.lsoft.com
www.mail-archive.com

Earlier, I recommended getting a second dial-up account with AOL or Compuserve in order to access their forums. When you log on to AOL or Compuserve, search for "forum" and then "craft".

Forums usually offer articles of interest to viewers. You can upload an article to these sites and be read by hundreds or thousands of browsers. Almost every forum will have a "recommended Web sites" page where you might post your announcement.

AOL and Compuserve (now owned by AOL) have different ways for posting to their forums. If your budget allows you to have accounts at both, then get involved with forums on the two services. If you have to choose between AOL and Compuserve because of expense, then go with AOL as it has far more subscribers, around 20 million.

Other online services have forums, too. However, getting accounts with all of them could be prohibitive. The way to tell if its worth your while is to measure your results from promoting on AOL first. If your sales are increasing from your promotion, start experimenting on different forums. See Chapter 14 to learn more about tracking your marketing results.

Participate in several lists until you locate those you feel are interested in your subject. Stick with moderated groups, they tend to be protected from SPAM. Here's how to get involved:

• Choose the right newsgroups for your art or craft. Most groups will not tolerate ads disguised as postings.

• Observe first. This is often referred to as 'lurking'. Read the postings for about a week before you post anything. This is the best way to learn what's appropriate for each group.

• Create catchy text for the subject line of your posting.

• Make your message brief, no more than will fit on a single screen.

• Re-post once a week on subjects you may have knowledge. It helps to research and formulate useful responses.

• Don't SPAM or post blatantly commercial messages. Determine ahead of time whether the list is likely to be open to your message.

• Offer something for free that has value, like an article, report, survey result, sample, book, audio tape, etc.

• Watch the postings to see how others responds. If you are helping a particular person, send them a personal email in addition to the group posting.

• When you become known to the group as a helpful person who offers good information, you will build a reputation and traffic to your site will increase.

• Introduce yourself to the host of the newsgroup, forum or mailing list. If you have something of interest to their list, they are likely to help you with your message to avoid getting flamed.

Join Internet clubs

Internet clubs are a lot like newsgroups. In fact, I can't tell much difference except that the word "club" may feel more cozy to some. Join as many online clubs related to your craft as you can. A search for "craft" at **clubs.yahoo.com** brought back 237 items. ("Witchcraft" anyone?) Another site with listings of clubs is at **www.theglobe.com**. Post messages to online clubs as you would a newsgroup or forum.

Chapter 10 How to Boost Your Traffic and Sales With Free Publicity

One of the most powerful, yet overlooked venues for promotion is free publicity, often referred to as PR, or public relations. Most small business owners do not make use of publicity channels because they don't know or understand its value.

First of all, publicity is free. Editors and reporters are busy people looking for news of interest to their readers. If a story about what you do is newsworthy, they will mention you, perhaps even write a one or two page feature article.

Second, an article or mention in a magazine will inspire more confidence than advertising. People know that companies pay for ads and that their agenda is to sell their products, so there is little trust. People trust what they read in articles, books, and news reports. Frankly, one look at the newspaper would make you wonder how this could be.

Overworked editors are happy to place your news story because it makes their job easier. I have found that many editors print my news releases verbatim, sometimes without calling me to confirm the facts which unfortunately can lead to problems.

One instance led to some unhappy readers. An over zealous reporter took information about a newsletter I published that appeared in *Working Mothers* magazine and reprinted it in their local newspaper without calling to confirm with me first that the newsletter was still available. The original news release I sent out was over two years old and by the time the story resurfaced, I no longer produced the newsletter. Of course, when this happens, you can offer callers something else of interest as long as you have them on the phone.

A great subject for publicity is an offer of something free. Readers love free stuff and editors are always looking out for free offers for their subscribers.

Using news releases

There are lots of ways to get traffic to your Web site. But just getting traffic isn't enough, you want to attract visitors who are interested in purchasing your craft.

The big advantage of using PR is that you can target publications and other media who already have the audiences you are trying to reach.

The more closely targeted your audience, the more success you will enjoy from your Web site.

When it comes to getting publicity, persistence is the key. Get your news releases in front of editors enough times and eventually they will take notice of you. For years, I sent news releases to 300 craft related magazines, including *Family Circle* whose subscriber base is around 10 million readers. They never called me back or printed any mention of me in their magazine. I almost took their contact info off my list. However, after sending releases to them for five years, one day a reporter from their *Holiday Crafts* issue called saying she wanted to interview me, from having seen one of my press releases. That interview resulted in about $3,000 in sales and a subsequent interview with them again next year.

News releases are a way to get news out about your site. You could write one every month on a different angle of your subject and keep the publicity ongoing. Of course, you want to make sure the receiving publication is interested in your topic.

In addition to a news release, you may want to send a press kit. A press kit can be a folder with your release, brochure, copies of other articles, awards and testimonies and a sample of your product. To get an idea of what press kits typically contain, browse the options at **www.presskits.com**.

Cost to you for writing articles and news releases

Your costs are your time and the expenses of printing and mailing the news release. Is it worth the effort? The news release mentioned above resulted in an interview with me in *Family Circle* magazine. *Vantage* magazine with around 500,000 subscribers wrote a full page article that brought in over $4,000 in orders.

What kind of returns can you expect for your Web site? In an Internet business, you are looking for visits to your site, email addresses you can add to your database and sales from your Web site. If your material offers something fresh or controversial, you will get many editors mentioning or featuring you. Be sure to include your Web site address in the release or article.

How to write news releases

News that is likely to get picked up and included by editors has a hook. That is, an idea or story that will catch attention. Look at examples of special interest stories appearing in newspapers and magazines for ideas. The hook doesn't have to be wild or exotic, it can relate to money, health, happiness, fears, controversy or current events. Does your craft site tie into anything happening in the news? If so, write a news release.

A news release should inform the publication of the who, what, where, when, why, and how of your story. Don't use words like "unique," "the best," "fantastic" or any other hype. Editors will toss your release in the trash. Write your story as a news event.

The form should be cleanly typed and double spaced. Use a heading with the name and title of the editor on the first line of the upper left corner all in caps. Follow this with the name of the periodical and then, a short title that tells something concise about your story. Include a release date or type "For Immediate Release." Skip down about four inches from the top of the page and place the heading for your release. Begin the news information under the heading.

Include these elements in the release, preferably in the first two paragraphs: who is it about, what is the event, when is it happening, where it is held, why is it newsworthy. Two to three paragraphs is plenty. Ideally, you want all the material to fit on one page or one viewer screen for online releases.

Include any past awards and accomplishments. Here is where you want to build yourself into an authority

At the end, center and type "-end-" or "###." Skip down two lines and then put "For more information, call: (your phone number)."

When you send a news release, include past reviews or articles about you along with photos of you at work. Send releases out frequently, say once a month to newspapers, magazines and online ezines with audiences interested in your subject.

The following release is an example. Not only is it brief and to the point, it offers readers free help, which is sure to get some news coverage. When this mention appears, persons interested in buying gifts from gourds will surely visit the Web site.

This release could be mailed to all women's magazines, general craft publications and local newspapers. If budget allowed, I would also mail it to major newspapers around the country.

NEWS RELEASE   From: Cindy Mill
                            15 Aztec St, Santa Fe NM 87341
                            Contact: Cindy Mill (505)402-3195

FOR IMMEDIATE RELEASE:

NEW WEB SITE PROVIDES FREE GOURD MAKING TIPS

A new Web site has just been opened called www.GourdMaker.com. The site offers free tips and resources for how to create decorative gourds as gifts. The Web site is authored by, Cindy Gourd, prize winning craft artist and educator. Www.GourdMaker.com also provides articles on the history of gourd craft and links to more resources on the Internet.

To access the free information on gourd making, visit the Web site, www.gourdmaker.com.

Cindy Gourd is a nationally recognized expert in gourd crafting. Winner of the 1999 Exhibit Prize at the New Mexico State Fair, she is the recipient of several awards for her work. Ms. Gourd has been featured in the Santa Fe New Mexican and Better Homes & Gardens.

·· END ··

/CONTACT: Cindy Mill, (505)402-3195

Writing articles

Writing articles is the cheapest most cost effective splash for your money. If you don't have a lot to spend on advertising, going for publicity through writing articles is the way to go. As an expert in your art or craft, you have knowledge or access to information that is of interest to audiences.

For instance, you may practice a craft that originated hundreds or thousands of years ago like weaving. Check the lists of ezine and newsletter directories in Chapter 8. You would also do a search at the directories and search engines for online forums, ezines, newsletters and magazines related to crafts or fiber arts and submit your article to the editor.

Most editors will allow you to include a "signature" that can point readers to your Web address. See more on signatures in the previous chapters.

I write articles regularly to publicize my business. You can too. Write one short article a month and send it to ezine editors who publish related materials. Writing for ezines is not hard. If you have something of interest to say about your art or craft, you will find an ezine willing to accept your articles.

Another avenue for promotion is to upload free articles to forums on the subject matter you are writing about. For instance, AOL and Compuserve have forums organized by subject categories. Many different topics are discussed. Often, you can also track the number of times each article was downloaded. Sites that host articles for use by editors and journalists include:

www.aracopy.com
certificate.net/wwio
www.ezinearticles.com
www.ideamarketers.com
www.web-source.net/articlesub.htm

Articles for ezines should be brief. Most run usually 300 to 500 words. Sentences should be short and newsy. Use a title that catches interest. Include a brief bio of you and a signature at the end with your URL. If you are writing for print publications, check their submission guidelines for article size and how to submit.

Keep a log of every place you upload an article online or get an article in print. This way when you need to change or update your information, you can find them easily. Keeping a record will help prevent you from uploading or submitting the same article to the same place more than once.

What to send editors

Although this may seem obvious, make sure your Web site is ready for intense scrutiny by professional editors before you do any PR to media. Double check your Web pages for spelling errors and broken links. Make sure the site has a consistent appearance when viewed by major browsers.

Experts disagree on exactly what is the best way to send news releases to editors. One thing seems certain, if you send the release on plain white paper to the postal address of the editor, you have a good chance it will get noticed.

If your news is urgent - and for most craft persons, this would be a stretch - send the release via fax. One recent survey reported that editors prefer receiving fax news releases to email or postal mail.

In the book, *Publicity on the Internet,* author and successful Internet publicist, Steve O'Keefe says sending news releases by email is not only okay, but recommended. O'Keefe reports success here is about creating relationships with the editors you are trying to reach, not indiscriminate mass mailings or SPAM.

His advice is to keep email news releases brief and catchy. Ideally, your message will fit on one screen view. You can and should always include a link to more material elsewhere. O'Keefe also recommends that if an editor requests to be removed from your list, that you do so.

Of course, if you are sending targeted news to specific editors, most will want to see the release. Don't waste your time sending news releases to inappropriate audiences. You'll just burn bridges before you are ready to cross them.

See the appendix for email addresses of media editors online to submit news releases and articles.

How to format an email news release

When you type an email message into your email manager program, text flows automatically to the next line down when you reach the end of the allowable space. Unfortunately, all email managers don't share the same standards as to what is the length of a line of type.

You've probably received emails where the lines look like someone went in and chopped up the message. Imagine sending your important news releases to editors and they see your message in short phrases that don't seem to connect.

For sending news releases that appear consistent in any email reader, the solution is to limit the lines of text to 60 characters. Compose the text of your email in a word processor using a 60 character line length. At the end of each line, place a hard return. Then save the message as an ASCII text file. Now import the text file into your email composer and send yourself the message to check for how it appears. Double check your release for spelling errors, typos, and contact information before sending to your media list.

Offline publicity

Print media editors, like online editors, are always on the look out for interesting articles and news for their readers.

There are over 11,000 magazines published in North America alone and over 200,000 editorial contacts for print and broadcast media. The directories listed below help you:

• See the number of issues per year.
• Locate target markets.
• Learn editorial deadline dates for receiving material.
• Identify special sections to target your niche audience.
• Learn the size of circulation, names of editors, advertising rates and editorial policies.

I recommend getting a list of possible publications that draw audiences you want to reach. Send a letter to each magazine on your company stationery requesting to receive their media kit for ad rates. You will shortly receive a free copy of their magazine and information on advertising which you will probably not need.

Go through each publication and look at subjects they cover and the kinds of articles included. Do the articles relate to your craft? Would your customers read this magazine? Will editors accept outside submissions? Does the magazine cover other craft persons? Does the magazine include mention of Web sites of interest? If you can answer yes to these questions regarding a publication, then place those in a stack to contact with your news releases and product information.

To locate directories of magazines, newspapers, syndicated columnists, and editors, see your library for these directories or visit the online sites:

Bacon's Media - **www.baconsinfo.com**
332 S. Michigan Ave, Chicago, IL 60604, 800-621-0561

Gebbie Press - **www.gebbieinc.com**
PO Box 1000, New Paltz NY 12561, 914-255-7560

Ulrich's International Periodical Directory -
www.bowker.com
R. R. Bowker, 121 Chanlon Road
New Providence, NJ 07974, 1-888-269-5372

The Newsletter Clearinghouse - (newsletter directory)
www.newsletter-clearinghse.com/index2.htm
P.O. Box 311, Rhinebeck, New York 12572
1-800-572-3451

Also see the appendix in this guide for a list of many online media contacts.

TV websites for publicity

TV may not be appropriate media for most craft persons because of the difficulties in handling large unexpected orders resulting from publicity. However, for those who can quickly organize and manage an operation that produces quantities of goods, TV interviews can help give you national exposure. If your site has a unique craft or newsworthy catch, try connecting to these TV Web sites with a news release:
* Aleene's - **www.aleenes.com**
* Better Homes & Gardens TV - **www.bhglive.com**

- Bob Vila's Home Site - **www.bobvila.com**
- Discovery Channel - **www.discovery.com/online.html**
- HGTV - Home and Garden TV - **www.hgtv.com**
- Lifetime TV - **www.lifetimetv.com**
- Martha Stewart Living - **www.marthastewart.com**
- QVC - **www.qvc.com**

Using a PR service

One of the first places to post your news release is at **www.prweb.com**. It's a free service that allows you to upload a news release that may get picked up by media editors hunting for stories.

If you don't have time to search and submit news releases yourself, there are services that do it for you. They are usually called public relations or PR firms. For a fee, they will create, edit, mail and submit your releases to targeted publications.

Here are firms that handle PR for clients with Web sites:

www.guestfinder.com

www.netpost.com

www.newsbureau.com/services

www.tenagra.com

An important benefit of PR is that it gets your name in front of people as an artist, craftperson, or expert in your field. The more recognizable your name becomes, the more likely people will buy your work and assign higher monetary value to your products.

Helpful resources for getting publicity

www.netrageousresults.com

www.actupny.org/documents/Media.html - Article: How to Handle Media

www.triangle.org/riskmgmt/media.html Article: Tips for Dealing with the Media

www.sev.com.au/webzone/webpubli.asp Tutorial: Online guide to Web promotion

Chapter 11 How to Use Online Auctions for Selling Your Craft

Auction sites online provide an excellent opportunity for craft sales. **Ebay.com** is the largest and most popular auction site with over 1.5 billion page views per month. There are many more auction sites you should check out as well. **Amazon.com** hosts auctions in addition to selling books, music, and anything else they can find.

One huge advantage of getting your products up on an auction site like Ebay is that they already get the traffic you want so badly - like 12 million customers or more. Cost to you is a small listing fee paid to the auction site plus a small commission when a sale is made.

A word of caution about using auction pages to send traffic to your own Web site. Ebay is aware of how companies might 'steal' traffic and has tightened their policies of linking to sites outside Ebay. They will only allow you to link to your web site IF the sole purpose of the page you're linking to is to provide the potential bidders with more photos and/or information about the item or items you are auctioning on ebay. See their site policies and procedures for details.

Of course, once visitors have arrived to your auction related information page, many of these new visitors may click through to your home page.

To become successful at marketing via auctions requires work, which means time and study in the start-up phase. For those who pursue auctions frequently, software exists to automate the time consuming tasks of posting auctions and recording results.

In the beginning, spend time visiting and reviewing the auction sites. Check out other artists and craft persons as well as their related Web sites. Study the search engines at **Ebay.com** and the other auction sites so that you understand how they work. Don't give up the first few times you run auctions and get poor results. It takes time to get a feel for how to make these sites work for you.

The auction phenomena is as much art as it is science and because online auctioning is still a relatively new phenomena in business, you may find yourself discovering selling techniques that no one else has used.

Types of auctions

Absolute auction - Products are sold to the highest bidder regardless of price. There is no minimum price set.

Minimum bid auction - In a minimum bid auction, a minimum price is set that you, the seller will accept for your product. This minimum amount is shown clearly on the auction page for bidders to see.

Reserve auctions - A reserve price is a specific price that you will absolutely not sell lower than. Bidders are aware there's a reserve price, but they do not have access to what it is. To win the auction, the bidder have submitted the high bid and must meet or go beyond the reserve price. Typically, when the reserve price is not met, the seller does not make the sale and the highest bidder is not obligated to buy.

In general, reserve auctions are not to your advantage. A reserve price is hidden to the bidders and is an amount you predetermine the bidding must meet to win. Most people avoid reserve price auctions because they have no idea what the value of the piece is. Start your prices at the lowest amount you will accept. If the item doesn't sell, start again at a lower price or list different items.

Dutch auctions - This type of auction is for selling multiple copies of the same item. An example would be 10 mugs, 17 sets of earrings or 25 pattern books. Sellers list an opening bid or minimum price along with the number of items for sale. Bidders enter the price they want to pay and the quantity to buy. All winning bidders pay the same price— the lowest successful bid.

Private auctions - This kind of auction protects a buyer's privacy. Bidders' email addresses are not displayed on the item or bidding-history screens. When the auction ends, the seller is the only one who knows the winner. Private auctions can't be tracked by the bidder and so, are less popular.

What auctions cost you

As a seller, you pay an insertion fee to list your item on an auction. Insertion fees range from $.25 to $10 or higher. When the item sells, you will be charged a value fee which ranges from 1% to 5% of the selling price.

To get your item listed in bold print or as a featured item, expect to pay additional charges. I recommend you avoid spending extra money in the beginning on listing features such as bold letters. Most people will find your auction because they are searching for keywords related to your product. You might attract a few viewers from a feature listing, but your most likely prospects for placing bids will be searchers looking for specific items.

Each auction is different in their fee structure, so read their terms carefully before starting.

How to sell at auctions

The following steps will get you to started on the auction sites. Take a look at what other craft artists are doing on **Ebay.com** as examples.

1. Draft a benefit laden description of your product. Gather all your images and text descriptions. Use graphic bullets to emphasize each benefit or feature.

2. Determine your minimum selling price. You may have to experiment at first. Learn what prices people will start bidding on. If you want help on pricing your craft work for wholesale or retail markets, see **www.craftmarketer.com/pricing-crafts.htm**.

3. Set up an account with the auction site. Each site has easy to follow instructions to guide you through the process.

4. Create your page(s) at the auction site(s) using your text descriptions and images.

5. Link to your website if your auction prices are not lower than prices shown on your Web catalog.

6. Decide which categories your item falls under - there should be several. Determine other areas your customers will visit and list there, too.

7. Save all the above info in a spreadsheet or database file or one of the software programs described later in this chapter.

8. Enter the auction site's "sell your item" page and fill out the appropriate forms. Each auction will require you to register as a seller with your own ID, user name and password.

9. You will get a confirmation page or email with a number for each auction you are posting. Write this number down or enter the number in your spreadsheet or software for tracking auctions.

10. When your auction closes, contact your winning bidder or bidders, usually within three business days. Confirm the final cost, including any shipping charges, and tell them where to send payment. When the bidder sends in payment to you, send them your item.

See **pages.ebay.com/help/sellerguide/selling-tips.html** for tips on selling at eBay.com.

More tips for auctions

• Try listing your items as regular auctions and dutch auctions to see which type of auction produces more sales and higher profits.

• Don't close your auction down early just because there are no bids. Many bidders wait until the last minute to bid.

• Make your emails to potential customers friendly and it will help you create a larger group of customers. A friend of mine who sells computer parts via auctions as a full time business tells me that because he has personalized his email responses to bidders, he has built up a regular base of customers who email him regularly with requests for new offers.

• Contact losing bidders by email and offer them a product at their high bid. You know they wanted the item because they took the time to bid. Creating a database of your bidders emails provides you a list of potential customers for new products, sale items and announcements.

• Mail invitations to your auctions to your existing customers by email or post cards. Offer free shipping, discount coupons off future auctions or purchases from your Web site, free promotional giveaways and any other promotional scheme that would motivate visitors to check out your auctions or Web site.

How to choose your subject categories

List your items in as many categories as possible. Doing so will maximize the number of bidders you get which in turn, drives up the bid price. Take some time to peruse the categories at the major auction sites. You'll probably come up with several ideas just browsing.

Don't limit yourself to categories under which your items obviously seem to fit. Look for more areas where customers go who would buy your items. For instance, if you produce handmade photo albums, one category to list under would be "Collectibles."

The more general the category, the more likely your auction will get lost. Try to get into specific categories. For example, say you make metal sculptures of dinosaurs. You would probably get bids listing under the following categories:

Collectibles: Crafts: Handcrafted Arts
Collectibles: Animals: Dinosaur
Collectibles: Animals: Reptile
Collectibles: Animals: Fantasy
Collectibles: Animals: Wildlife
Collectibles: Animation Art
Collectibles: Art: Fine: Sculptures
Collectibles: Metalware
Collectibles: Decorative
Collectibles: Science Fiction: Godzilla
Collectibles: Miscellaneous

Although auction sites have their own search engine under which buyers search for what they want, users are likely to go to one of the category headings first and continue narrowing their search before they use the search engine. This means the category heading is your first group of potential bidders.

For example, in an Ebay auction you would list silver jewelry under the main category "Gemstones/Jewelry." Then you could further target visitors within that category by listing under "Jewelry: Silver: Designer, Signed."

Bidders will also come from your item description which contains keywords, buyers search for. Therefore, construct your item's description using your most important keywords. Since searchers will follow the category headings toward "Jewelry: Silver: Designer, Signed," there is no need for you to include those keywords in your description. Instead, you might write a description with keywords like "sterling", "necklace", or your name as the designer. This method of listing allows you to get the most lookers from an efficient use of keyword descriptions.

Feedback ratings

Most auctions have feedback ratings for buyers and sellers. Feedback ratings, positive ones that is, are the most important way of conveying trust to the potential customers who don't know you. For sellers, you can check up on your bidders to see if they have a history of not paying after winning bids.

Locate auctions

The following is a list of the major auction sites. Each site has its own rules but once you become familiar with how one online auction works, you will find it easier to post to other sites.

Top auction sites:
www.ebay.com
www.amazon.com
auctions.yahoo.com
www.auctionport.com
auctions.lycos.com
www.biddingtons.com

More auctions:
www.aaands.com
www.auctionaddict.com
www.auctions.com
www.auctionware.com
www.bidmore.com
www.bidz.com
www.boxlot.com

www.cityauction.com

www.collectorsauction.com

www.edeal.com

www.popula.com

www.playle.com

www.utrade.com

Because of the rapid changes in the Internet industry, it pays to keep up with trends and reviews of auction sites. Check out the following sites that offer newsletters and articles:

www.auctionwatch.com

www.auctioninsider.com

www.auctiontalk.com

auctiontribune.com

www.internetauctionlist.com

Organizing your auction business

As your auction sales grow, you will find yourself inundated by emails from customers, shipping invoices and more details. Organize your growing work flow with:

• A set of standard or canned email replies ready for commonly asked questions such as the terms shown on your auction. Yes, people will ask you for information that is clearly available on your pages.

• Specific payment and shipping terms should be listed clearly in your auction. For instance, who pays shipping? What methods of payment will you accept - money order, credit cards, personal checks, etc.? Will you ship outside the U.S.? Do you provide insurance? See the tip on self insurance at the end of this chapter.

• Organize fulfillment so that all orders can be packed and shipped quickly. Have your shipping supplies, labels and a postage meter or scale.

• Record all auctions to measure results.

Software for use with auction sites

To be successful with auctions, you must post multiple auctions and post frequently. Multiple posting by hand would be a logistical nightmare so here are alternatives that will save you time and money.

For listing multiple items or many auctions, you can save descriptions in a word processing or notebook file, then cut and paste text to the "list your auction" pages at the auction sites.

Ebay, Amazon, Yahoo and UAuction provide "bulk loaders" that use a table for loading multiple items. Other software programs accomplish bulk loading to auctions. Here is a list:

AuctionPoster - **www.auctionposter.com**
AuctionAssistant - **www.blackthornesw.com**
Auction Submit - **www.auctionsubmit.com**
AuctionTrackerBrowser - **www.auction-browser.com**
Auctiva Manager - **www.auctiva.com/products/eb.asp**
Bidmaster - **bay-town.com**
BidTracker - **bidtracker.borrell.com**
Ebay Assistant - **ebassistant.hypermart.net**
Merlin Bulk Lister - **www.pctechzone.com/bulklister**
www.powerlister.com/powerlister_ebay.html
reSale - **re-ware.com**

When looking at auction software, check for the following functions:
• automatic online entry of multiple listings
• write ad copy once, then recycle it
• conduct large number of sales campaigns a day

Shipping, handling and insurance fees

In most mail order transactions, the buyer pays for shipping. The same is generally true for auction purchases. If you scan several listings in the auctions, you will find a variety of shipping and handling charges from various vendors. Some sellers try to raise their profits by adding on handling charges. I recommend you don't try to profit through inflated shipping costs. Auction shoppers are looking for bargains and they recognize exorbitant shipping costs.

For recovering your shipping and handling expenses, include a high enough shipping price that you are reimbursed for your postage, envelope, any protective foam or wrapping and your auction commissions.

Another approach is to include these charges in the amount you set as the opening bid price for the item and offer free shipping. Put the words **"free shipping"** in bold letters on your auction description and you will get more bids.

Try both of the above methods and track the results. If you see a measurable drop in sales where you have raised the opening bids, you may get better results from adding the handling charges into the shipping amount.

When you become adept at selling through auctions, you will run multiple auctions at the same time. Consider adding a statement on your item description that the buyer will save on shipping costs of several items if they win more than one auction. Remember that auction bidders are looking for the best deal or they wouldn't be bidding.

To help you estimate shipping charges via the most popular carriers, these companies provide online quote calculators:

iShip.com from Ebay - **iship.com/ebay/seller.asp**

UPS (United Parcel Service) - **ups.com/using/services/rave/rate.html**

USPS (U.S. Postal Service) - **postcalc.usps.gov**

FedEx (Federal Express) - **www.fedex.com/us/rates**

Self-insurance

Consider offering an additional charge for insurance. Suppose you gave your customer an option of paying $1 for extra insurance. If your products are not easily damaged in shipping, you could earn extra money from those who elect to pay the insurance charge. The money would go into your own "self-insurance" fund. Odds are that you will always have more money coming into the fund than going out to pay for replacements.

Counters for auction pages

Using counters on your auction pages will help you track how many people are looking at your offer. You can experiment with using different graphics, promotional text and minimum bids to learn what offers draw more visitors. You can get auction page counters at **www.honesty.com** and **count.rubylane.com** .

Selling craft supplies

When you buy supplies for making your craft, you probably look for wholesale prices and special deals whenever possible. Put your excess supplies up for sale on auction sites. This could easily grow into a profitable second income stream for you. Some craft persons are experiencing great success with this. There a lot more people making crafts than looking to buy handcrafted work. An estimate of persons involved in craft is anywhere between 6 and 10 million people based on subscriptions to craft magazines. What if you got 1/10 of 1% of those as customers for your craft supplies? That would be 6,000 to 10,000 prospects!

Pricing

What is the best selling price range for your work sold on auction sites? If you make something that can be sold for between $5 and $20, you will do well. Higher priced items do sell, but you wait longer between sales than if you have a supply of items priced $20 or less.

What if you only sell higher priced items? On **Ebay**'s search page, I ran a search for the word "craft" to be found in the title and description of the auction. I specified a price range between $20 and $500. The results totaled 1,284 auctions, many of which had bids shown. So yes, high priced crafts sell at auction sites, too. In fact, almost anything will sell at online auctions. Just browse **Ebay's** categories for examples.

For getting new customers, consider selling low cost items as loss leaders, that is, selling items at a loss in order to get customers for higher ticket items you introduce after the initial sale. A link from the auction page could lead them to your Web site. Or, include a flyer with the first purchased item when shipping it to the buyer.

If your aim is to generate direct sales with a specific profit margin, you will need to figure in all your costs and price your work so that you recover those costs. Don't forget to add in a profit margin.

For help on different ways to use pricing techniques, see ***The Basic Guide to Pricing Your Craftwork***, ($12.95 from 1-800-235-6570).

Amazon's zshops

Zshops from Amazon are not auctions, but can be set up to work with your auctions at Amazon. The program is great for merchants selling items in quantities. The zshop marketing concept allows you to put up a store front through Amazon to reach the company's 12 million plus buyers. The program requires a listing fee from 24 cents to $2 and percentage of sale fee of 1.5% to 5% of the sale depending on the price.

Another advantage of using zshops is that Amazon will allow buyers to purchase from you and use Amazon's merchant account to pay. Amazon's name for the system is called "OneClick." You pay a small commission for using their OneClick - around 5% of the sale, but this is an affordable alternative to setting up your own merchant account to accept credit cards. For details, go to **www.amazon.com**.

Chapter 12 How to Make Money With Affiliate Programs

Affiliate or associate programs pay commissions to Web sites which refer visitors to their products or services who make a purchase. This chapter describes how you can profit from setting up your own affiliate program or through joining another company's program.

You can create an affiliate program for your crafts or related products whereby others promote your product on their Web site and you pay them a commission for every sale. This is like creating your own referral or network marketing program.

Another way to profit from associate programs is to join someone else's plan and display links or ads to their product on your site. They pay you a commission on every sale. It is quite possible to earn a couple of hundred to several thousand dollars extra income through participating in affiliate programs. One of the keys to success is promoting a product or service that you use and enjoy yourself. Your own written testimonial is more persuasive than a banner ad.

Jupiter Communications, a widely respected forecaster of Internet trends, predicts that by 2002, one fourth of all retail sales online will originate on affiliate sites.

Setting up your own affiliate program

Since you create your products, you know the costs involved and how much profit you can afford to share with associate partners. The only way the deal will work for you is if the margin between the retail and your actual costs allows you to give at least 20% to associates. Commissions for less than 20% will most likely fail to attract and motivate many associates. Again, if you need help determining your profit margins, see *The Basic Guide to Pricing Your Craftwork*.

Another requirement for setting up an affiliate program is that you have your own domain name. You will want the domain name in order to set up affiliate home pages that look exactly like your product pages but have the referring associate's ID code so that you know where each referral is coming from.

One of the keys to making an affiliate program profitable is to choose associates with a related customer base. That is, if you were looking for dealers of your stained glass angels, you would approach or market to Web sites with angel themes.

For example, let's say your stained glass angel retails for $25. You offer affiliates 20% commission, or $5, for each angel bought through someone clicking on a banner or link to your site from the referring associate's site. Coding in the HTML identifies each visitor who comes to your site from others.

Even if your referring partners don't make any sales after several months, you have not lost anything because the program brought free advertising for your site.

You can market affiliate programs through a variety of ways including graphic image links, text links, autoresponders, classified ads and ezines. Because some browsers don't download graphic files if the viewer chooses that option, you want text and other links as alternatives. Browsers don't filter out text.

How to pay your associates

There are several ways to set up your commission pay-outs. The first and best method is to share a percentage of each sale with the referring associate. As in the example of the glass angel, a referring site will earn 20% of each sale.

Another way of paying for referrals is for associates to have customers fill in a form which is emailed to you. For each lead you receive, you pay the referrer a set fee. Similarly, you could pay associates for each click-through visitor that follows a link to your site.

I don't recommend paying for leads as it is too easy for others to cheat by falsifying click-throughs. Since click-through rates for banners have been steadily dropping in general, this method is not a good option. Also, just because someone clicks on a banner that takes them to your site, there is no assurance that they will make a purchase. By sharing sales commissions with your affiliates, your expenses are based on real purchases, a more measurable value.

Do-it-yourself associate management

In setting up your own pages for selling through a network of associates, each partner will get a mirror site of your company page. If your domain was www.angelsglass.com, then your first associate might have a page called www.angelsglass.com/af1.htm and the next one might be called www.angelsglass.com/af2.htm and so on.

Setting up pages for each affiliate will take some time as you have to imbed an ID in each of the pages HTML that identifies that affiliate when orders come in. When you set up the affiliate pages yourself, there is no cost involved but your hours.

The disadvantage is that when you get lots of associates, you spend many hours setting up and maintaining these mirror sites. Also, if you make changes to your main page, you have to go back and change all of your associates' pages. What happens to your schedule when you reach forty, fifty or more affiliates?

Software for managing your affiliate programs

A more practical means of handling your associate program is software or a service provider that automates the entire operation. Attempting to manage all the tasks by hand will only work in the beginning when you have a small number of associates.

Associate or affiliate management software programs organize and report on sales, click-throughs, commissions and Web pages of associates.

To locate affiliate software providers, do search for "affiliate software." Most programs I have seen are fairly expensive - from $200 to $750. An excellent list of resources is at: **2-tier.com**

Service companies that manage affiliate programs

Service providers can set up and manage your program for you through a Web site that automates the tasks of enrolling new members and tracking commissions. Of all the options, for running an associate program, this plan offers you the most freedom and the fastest set up time.

Here is a list of affiliate service managers:

www.affiliateshop.com

www.cj.com

www.clicktrade.com

www.linkshare.com

www.reporting.net

What to provide affiliates

The following list includes basic functions that will increase the rate of sign ups for your associate program. Whether you are managing the program yourself or using a software or service provider, you want the following:

Automated enrollment. Software or service provider should create easy forms for affiliates to enroll. An autoresponder should go out giving them details on getting banners or text links and how to use them.

Mass email should be easily distributed. You want the ability to email all your affiliates easily and quickly. For instance, you might have developed a new way of marketing your product they could implement and increase their sales.

Operations should be accessible by you. You should be able to make changes to fees, check commission status, pay referral fees, and change all associate pages at once.

Automated statistics. Software should be able to track orders from online, your toll free number, fax orders, and orders arriving in the mail. Your affiliates should be able to check their statistics at any time, seeing how many sales and click through's are coming through.

Pay-outs. Software should be able to handle automatic check writing of commissions.

Making money from other affiliate programs

Even if you don't feel your craft product lends itself to referral marketing, there are plenty of income opportunities available by participating in other affiliate programs.

To be profitable, however, you should have some experience with the product or service you are recommending. The most successful affiliates are those who have experienced exciting benefit from the use of the product.

When you have used a software product or service or piece of hardware you really liked and could write a heartfelt testimonial about, check with that product's maker about affiliate sales opportunities. Many sites now have links to their referral programs. Most of them cost nothing to join.

Another important ingredient is that customers that know and trust you personally are ten times more likely to buy a product you recommend. With referral marketing, you simply tell your own experience with something that may have changed your life for the better.

Where to find affiliate or associate programs

The sites mentioned earlier as affiliate service providers also list their existing programs, usually displayed in a directory format that allows you to browse for deals that might suit your marketing aims. Also check the home pages on sites that you visit for a link to their affiliate program. Here are other sites for locating revenue sharing programs for your site. Most of these sites offer a free email newsletter that keeps you up to date on succeeding at affiliate deals.

www.2-tier.com

www.associateprograms.com

www.befree.com

www.cj.com

www.internet.com/affiliates/index.html

www.refer-it.com/main.cfm

webmaster-programs.com

Chapter 13 How to Buy and Sell Online Advertising

Buying and selling advertising is another avenue for generating traffic and sales. However, you may well ask yourself *"why spend the money, when there are so many free options for marketing online?"* When buying advertising generates additional sales that pay you more than the expense of the ads, then it is worth the cost.

Although Internet advertising may be inappropriate for most craft businesses, this chapter will prepare you for the day when your site generates the kind of traffic advertisers look for - that is a minimum of 10,000 unique visitors a month. Also, there may be opportunities to promote your site through purchasing ads at high traffic sites with visitors like those you wish to attract.

One reason to understand how online advertising works and why you may someday want to make use of ads is that the Internet is becoming more commercialized every day. As the large corporations move online, they tend to function the way they do offline, that is, with advertising dollars. Search engines that were mostly free vehicles for posting your site with are now owned by major corporations. Some examples are Compaq owns DEC which owns Alta Vista; NBC owns part of Snap; Disney purchased major shares of Infoseek. Don't panic though, these search engines are still free.

This chapter will give you both sides of the coin for understanding and utilizing the different kinds of Internet advertising, for using ads to promote your site and getting ad revenue from your site.

Classified ads to promote your site

There are hundreds of sites you can post free classified ads promoting your product and Web site. Most of them will result in little additional traffic. However, if you post your URL in classified ads, they may add to your popularity with search engines, thus boosting your own page rankings.

You can do a search on any engine and come up with lots of sites. Here are some free classified ad sites especially for arts and crafts:

> **wwar.com/classpro/newad.html**
> **www.sherlonscraftmall.com/links/links.html**
> **www.usa5.com/class/class1.htm**
> **naia-artists.org**
> **www.ppi-free.com**
> **www.gems4friends.com/classifieds/index.html**

Warning: Whenever you post classified ads with your email address, you will receive unsolicited email from advertisers who use harvesting software that scans the Internet for addresses. Unfair? Yes, but you have a defense. Before placing your ads, set up several emails with the free email services mentioned earlier. Examples are **hotmail.com**, **yahoo.com** and many others. Include the free service email address in your ad instead of your main email. Or you could use an autoresponder with a free report that links to your URL. This way even those who SPAM you get your ad in return.

Paid classifieds in targeted ezines are more likely to increase your traffic. Readers have specifically requested subscriptions to the publication whose subject matter relates to what your selling. Check out the ezine sources listed in Chapter 8. Subscribe to several ezines and study them to get an idea of what kind of audience they have. Are readers primarily into collecting, art or craft history, health, herbs, pets, or business?

Know your target audience before spending money advertising. When you have a list of target publications, find out how big the readership is, how frequently it is published and the cost to run your ad.

Classified ads in ezines are usually inexpensive compared to classifieds in newspapers and magazines. It's possible to reach several hundred thousand or more targeted prospects with your ad costing less than $100.

If you want to advertise your Web site through classified ads in offline newspapers, you can get a bulk listing price with this service: **store.yahoo.com/classifieds/index.html**.

Ads at online services like AOL and Compuserve

Online services like AOL and Compuserve charge a monthly rate for access. Since those who use these services are accustomed to paying for information, they are better prospects for your ads. Compuserve is a good starting place to test your ad for effectiveness because their subscribers tend to be responsive to ads. You have to have a **Compuserve** account to get in. You may also want to set up a cheap dial-up account with **AOL** to make use of their classified sections. AOL had around 17 million subscribers in late 1999.

How to write your classified ad

Write your ad to attract prospects and entice them to visit your Web site. Use attention getting headlines that motivate the reader to act. These ads should not try to sell your products directly but rather get your reader to click on your URL and go to your Web site. At your site, visitors can read your marketing copy similar to what you might use in a direct mail letter selling your products. As mentioned earlier, this is called the two-step approach, a tactic you should use in all your online marketing. People are in a hurry. Just give them enough of a tease to click on a link to another Web page where you have already set up a longer marketing message which does the selling job.

Use power words in your headlines and subject lines. Certain words have proven to be more powerful than others to influence a reader. Experts employ these words to motivate the public to purchase their products. You can make use of these words too. Among the more effective words are:

> *new, you, now, riches, bargain, bonus, complete,*
> *easy, enjoy, exclusive, fast, free, help, love, proven,*
> *save, secret, special, success, today, yes, amazing,*
> *compare, power, quick, how-to, important, last*
> *chance, magic, startling, why, when, hurry,*
> *announcing, improvement.*

Books on the subject of direct marketing and mail order like *Building a Mail Order Business* by William Cohen list these and other response motivators.

Selling classified ads

Having a classified ad section on your site is a great way to get visitors to return. You can set up a page on your site to list classified ads for free or for a fee. How much you can charge depends on your traffic and the credibility of your site. There are thousands of sites for posting free ads, so you may not get many people willing to pay you to place an ad.

However, if you publish an ezine or newsletter, you can successfully charge for placements in a classified section of the letter. Since everyone who subscribes to your letter is opt-in, they won't mind the ads. In many online newsletters I receive, there are classifieds. Reports show these paid ads bring in better response rates from viewers than most of the free ad sites. This is because the subject matter of the letter is of particular interest to the reader. See Chapter 8 on ezines.

How to set up a classified section on your site

You can set up a classified section by hand, but the tasks take time. Adding in new listings and deleting the expired ads may not be worthwhile. These activities can be automated by software that sets up your ad pages and manages incoming placements, automatically setting expiration dates for each ad. By having limitations on the duration of ads, you motivate the person writing the ad to come back to your site again and again. Viewers also return to see the latest ads. Here's a list of resources for setting up a classified ad section on your site:

www.theadnet.com/member/webmaster.asp -- AdNet is a free service requiring no sign up hassles or fees. They provide you with a simple HTML code that allows insertion of your Web site URL giving the appearance that you are providing a huge selection of classified ads. Behind the scenes, AdNet's database of classifieds is doing the work.

www.e-classifieds.net -- E-classified software comes in several price ranges.

Sponsorships

Sometimes you will see the phrase "support our sponsors" on a Web site or included in a newsletter. Although one can argue that any ad is a sponsorship, this term refers to long term relationships where there might be a vested interest in the success of the Web site by funding organizations or capital investors.

Since some people have an aversion to "advertising", using the term "sponsorship" might improve viewers' impressions.

Sponsorship ads are more frequently seen in email mailing lists or ezines. Since readers of these lists are opting to receive the information, the viewers are more targeted audience and you should be able to charge more for sponsorship ads than you would on a Web site.

How to sell advertising on your site

If you can generate huge volume of visitors, you can sell advertising on your site. The amount of money you can charge and expect to receive for advertising is related to:
- Number of visitors/traffic to your site
- Frequency of hits
- Who your visitors are
- What your site is about
- Nature of the ads displayed

Banner ads will take your visitors directly to the site's URL nested in the banner graphic. Though banners may be the most effective way to sell ads from your site. However, displaying banner ads provides your visitor an escape route leading away from your site which may not be in your best interest.

Before you can begin selling banner ads, find your Web site's potential appeal to advertisers. Your site should have been up for at least six months to a year and getting 10,000 unique visitors or more per month. Most advertisers will not invest in small traffic sites.

Advertisers will choose your site because of the interests of your visitors. For instance, if you sell woodworking items, you might attract the interest of woodworking suppliers. Advertisers look for sites with similar topics to their ad message. Even so, you want to be able to demonstrate or describe how advertising on your site will generate traffic volume for the advertiser.

The more clearly defined your audience, the easier it will be to identify and attract potential ad clients. Stay away from offensive content for your site. Most companies will not want to be associated with "adult" content unless that is their business.

Companies are unlikely to advertise with you if you don't have your own domain. For instance, your site might look well designed but unlikely to generate ad revenue if it is hosted at one of the free host sites like geocities.com or tripod.com. Also, many of the free Web hosting sites prohibit selling ad space.

Banner ad effectiveness

Some reports indicate banners are being increasingly ignored. A Forrester Research statistic showed that 69% of banner clickers can't remember the last banner they clicked on.

A survey conducted by Wirthlin Worldwide of 1,000 adults found that 80% of Net users usually ignore Internet banners, but six out of 10 report having clicked through at least once.

On the other hand, there are examples of banner ad power. The average click-through for online banner ads featuring coupons is 20%, compared to the more typical 0.25% for standard banner ads

What makes people click on banners? One study showed that the chief reason was recognition or trust in a brand name or product. The next leading reason to click was a free offer of something. Following those reasons, in the order of their importance, people clicked for an interactive learning experience, humor or fun, stimulating graphic or music, and research to make a purchase. (from Wirthlin research.)

One survey of 1,500 Internet users indicated that 25% went shopping on a Web site after seeing a banner ad. This compared with 14% that went to a site because of a mention on television or in a magazine ad. Forrester Research showed banner ads were most effective when the product was associated somehow to the subject of the Web site. In other words, the more targeted the ad, the higher the click-through.

Does your site design support banner placements?

Do your pages have space for banner ads? If not, you will have to redesign them to accommodate the typical banner ad which is 468 x 60 pixels. Some Web authoring packages like FrontPage allow you to easily create rotating ad banners. This allows for many different banners to rotate at frequent intervals. You may want additional software to track the click through rate for each banner, although many of the banners from advertisers will have that capability built in.

Where to place banner ads for greatest click-through

Several studies show how banner position on the Web page affects click-through rates. One report showed that ads placed next to the right scroll bar - in the lower right-hand corner of the first page opened - generated a 228% higher click-through rate than ads placed at the top of that page. So, if you are selling something from the banner ad, put the link at the bottom right of the first screen. The same report showed that ads placed 1/3 down page, instead of at the top, generated only 77% higher click-through rates.

How much to charge for ads

To get an idea of what other sites charge, visit sites that sell advertising. You will know which sites they are because they usually have a link which you can click to get their rate card via email.

One industry average is around $35 per thousand views of an ad at smaller sites. However, more specialized information sites with very targeted viewers charge much higher rates. Say that you have 20,000 visitors per month at your website and your site has 20 pages, each with information of some kind. For a site with that traffic, you could charge $250 a month for a banner ad on each of the 20 pages. If you got 20 advertisers, one for each page, you would generate $5,000 a month.

To check out ad rates for sites which might be similar to yours or get a bigger picture of the Internet advertising industry and rates:

www.srds.com

www.adbase.net

www.adbility.com

Finding ad buyers

You can post a link and a page on your site with your ad rates for visitors to inspect. Don't expect much response in the beginning days of your Web presence. As your traffic grows and you generate consistent site traffic history, your attractiveness to advertisers will increase. Advertisers will want to know your traffic volume before deciding to spend money on ads at your site. Some will want to pay only on a click-through basis.

When your product appeals to a niche audience, you can approach owners of sites which also attract customers like yours about buying or trading ad space on your site.

Handling ad sales

Following are some guidelines for managing ad sales online:
- Create and use a written advertising agreement/contract with your terms clearly stated.
- Create an online and print version of your ad rates.
- Ask for payment in advance.
- If an advertiser wants credit terms, check their credit first.
- Accept credit cards as payment.
- Keep records of all transactions should legal action occur.

How to use an ad broker

Because of the time involved, selling ad space at your site is a task best delegated to a broker. Few of the larger more successful sites do their own ad hawking.

With all the large companies now online, it can be challenging to locate a broker or ad service bureau that is right for your business.

Many will want an exclusive agreement claiming they can do a better job than nonexclusive ad reps. However, this is not usually true. You are better off not signing such agreements except under limited time period, like six months to a year.

When interviewing prospective brokers, ask for references. Contact other ad buyers to learn their company's experience working with the broker. You can also learn if any companies have written about their experiences with brokers in one of the newsletters for online advertising. See the end of this chapter.

Companies that will help you find ad buyers for space on your site when you have the traffic:

www.adbility.com
www.realmedia.com
www.burstmedia.com
www.doubleclick.net

Pay for keywords

Overture.com is a search engine where companies bid on keywords. The highest bidder gets his Web site shown when visitors click on a keyword he has bid on. For instance, I did a search for the word "craft" at the Overture.com site. The first listing at the top of the search results page was a company called *PC Flowers Holiday Delivery*. At the end of their listing was the figure ($.49). This is the amount they pay for each visitor who clicks through to their site from Overture.com. To stay in business, *PC Flowers* must earn more than $.49 per visitor.

How do you know if it's worth paying for click-throughs? Divide your average visitors per month into your total sales per month and you then know the value of each visitor. If you don't have any visitors or any sales than I recommend you use all the free methods like search engines and links from other sites to generate traffic first before investing money in pay for click-through programs because newer sites without a traffic history can't be sure what percentage of visitors will become customers.

For news on trends in online advertising

To keep up with Internet advertising industry changes, visit **www.adbility.com**

Newsletters:

The Online Advertising Newsletter - **www.o-a.com**

The Advertising Networks mailing list -- To subscribe, send email to: **adnet-l-subscribe@egroups.com**.

Web Site Banner Advertising Digest -- To subscribe, send email to: **wsba-digest-subscribe@egroups.com**

The Affiliate Advertising mailing list -- To subscribe, send email to: **affiliate-l-subscribe@egroups.com**

The Clickthrough Advertising Mailing list -- To subscribe, send email to: **click-l-subscribe@egroups.com**

The Banner Exchange mailing list -- To subscribe, send email to: **bannerexchange-l-subscribe@egroups.com**

Advertising Results discussion list -- To subscribe, send email to: **adresults-l-subscribe@egroups.com**

Chapter 14 Measuring Your Results

How do you know if your efforts, time and money spent promoting online are successful? Sales are easy to track. Just count up the number of sales that come through your shopping cart. Divide the total of your sales dollars by the number of unique visitors for the same period to learn the dollar value of each visitor.

Measuring site traffic needs more attention. You want to know how many unique visitors you are getting to each page and you want to know which of your marketing efforts they are coming from. Otherwise, you might be spending hours promoting in noneffective ways.

When you know what pages are getting viewed or ignored, you can adjust your site accordingly. Pages that get looked at more often will be candidates for adding more product information, affiliate links or ads. Pages that aren't getting traffic can be dropped or modified experimentally.

Once you have a way to gather information about your Web site traffic and sales, the most useful way to organize your data is through creating a database. A database is like a big filing cabinet with folders holding names and addresses. The file folders can be organized instantly in any order you wish to facilitate creating mailing labels, invoices, reports and other useful output.

What to learn from tracking

• Number of impressions - impressions are the number of times a page or image is downloaded. Impressions are often confused with "hits". Hits are the number of elements downloaded by the user. A page with three graphics could count as four hits when viewed.

• Number of visitors - If a person views a page on your site, he is considered a visitor. However, if that person comes back two or three times later the same day, most tracking software counts him as a second or third visitor. It helps to qualify visits by "unique visitor." Many Web hosts or services mentioned later supply you with this info.

• Pages viewed - as mentioned earlier, if you can measure which pages are getting looked at, you can design your site for optimal performance.

• Visits broken down by hour, day, week and month.

• Average number of visitors per day.

• Length of stay - track how long a visitor spends on any given page.

• Point of origin - referrer logs provides information on the exact URLs of sites that refer visitors to you. You can track the effectiveness of promotional efforts and links you have arranged from other sites. If you get visits from sites you haven't set up links with, you can contact referring sites to create a relationship.

• You can also track visitors from other countries to learn if you should create your site in a foreign language version.

• Which browsers are being used to view your site. This helps you to learn how to design your pages for best viewing.

How to use the data you get from tracking

• See how your promotional efforts generate more traffic. For instance, you could have dozens of different doorway pages that allow access to your site. Each doorway page's URL could be the subject of a news release or advertisement in different magazines. After the news item or ad is published, look at your access logs and measure which magazine readers responded to your material or ad. For example, say that you want to run 17 classified ads for a gift basket offer. First create a new directory folder on your Web site called "/special." Then, create 17 pages to correspond to seventeen ads. Pages could be named www.yourname.com/special/gbc1.htm, www.yourname.com/special/gbc2.htm and so on. The "gbc" code might stand for "gift basket classified." Now you can track each ad's responses by checking page visits for each of these 17 pages.

Suppose you wanted to run a similar offer in an ezine or other avenue. Just change the coding slightly and keep a log of which pages correspond to which ads. Such a log can easily be created in a database program.

If you were doing an email direct letter to your customer base with an offer of a discount on a specific product offer, you could include an offer number that identifies call-in orders or online orders as coming from that email offer. Place the responses in your database to track the number of orders from that offer. If you are testing different email offers, you can track how each pulls.

Page counters

Page counters can be installed on your home page and the other pages throughout your site to measure visitor numbers. If you use counters, I recommend "hiding" them so that only you can see the results. What function does it serve to show your visitors your traffic information? Imagine the impression on your prospective customers when they see your counter showing "total number of visitors this year at 107." Low visitor numbers speak poorly of the Web site.

By placing hidden counters on every page, you can measure how people find your site. You can also measure which of your pages are getting looked at and which are being ignored. I've used this information to help assess what visitors are really looking for at my site and consequently improved the site's navigation.

Where to get free counters

beseen.com/beseen/free/counters.html
counters.virtualave.net
www.digits.com
www.fg-a.com/counter.htm
www.tonsilhockey.com/webdocs
www.iyp.org/counter/index.html
www.linkexchange.com/fastcounter
www.webmasterutilities.com

Site statistics from your Web host

A good Web host will provide you with a user log of your access statistics. If your Web host doesn't provide such statistics, consider moving. You should be able to learn how many visitors arrived to your site, which pages they saw, where they originated from, and how many times and where on your site visitors encountered "error messages" like "page not found." Additionally, you should be able to learn which keywords were used to find your site. Most Web hosts don't provide keyword statistics but you can get that information with Web Position Gold.

Tracking services online

If your host doesn't provide site traffic statistics and you don't want to move to another host, you can receive traffic reports through various outside sources, some for free, some at a cost.

Free tracking services may be unreliable because they are hosted on servers you have no access to. More reliable services are usually fee based. However, one of the most comprehensive free trackers is at: **www.extreme-dm.com/tracking.** This program will give you a report on the actual keywords used to find your site. Another free service is **www.counterguide.com** .

The following Web sites perform online tracking services at varying rates:

www.idstat.com/counter
www.counterguide.com
www.hitslink.com
www.digits.com
www.webtrends.com/products/default.htm

Tracking software

If you prefer not to use a service provider for tracking results, you can get software that analyzes your server logs and tracks your visitors with various amounts of data:

www.accesswatch.com
www.hitbox.com

Setting up a database

One of the most important functions your Web site can perform next to creating a sale is to capture and store customer contact information. Having a list of email addresses of your visitors allows you to send follow-up email letters on a regular basis at no cost.

The following example shows fields of data that might be included in a database. Once you enter the information in each field, you can sort by name, address, state or any other field. You can also create mailing labels, import and export data to other programs and many other useful tasks.

There are several database software programs, most of which come with tutorials. **Microsoft Access** and **FilemakerPro** are two popular and easy to use database programs and widely available at computer stores and online.

Picture of a database screen:

Date	Firstname	Lastname	Address1	Address2	City	State	Z
7/2/2000	Alex	Vase	123 Cherry St		Houston	TX	7707
7/4/2000	Sheryl	Brown	3 St Martin Pl		Austin	TX	7788
7/4/2000	Georgene	Fellows	23087 Che Blvd		Seattle	WA	9870

Final note

Many small business owners never envision the day they might sell their home grown enterprise. If they did, they might do more planning to make the business attractive enough that buyers would become interested. Usually it is larger companies that include an exit strategy in their plans.

With a Web site business, an exit strategy is not only feasible but potentially very lucrative. Despite the number of dot com failures, there are still billionaires who started Web site businesses from their garage. CDNow, Amazon, Yahoo, and even Microsoft began as small enterprises from the owners' homes. If there ever was a medium for business where you have an equal opportunity with the giants, it is the Internet.

Should you be building toward the day when you want to sell your Web site business, here are companies that broker domain names and Web sites:

www.domainmart.com - A market to register, buy, sell, and lease your online business, or domain name.

www.domainreseller.com - Helps you buy, sell, trade or lease your domain names.

www.websitebroker.com - Web site broker helps in buying, selling or trading existing Web sites. You can list your website for sale for free in their database or search the list of available sites.

Stay up to date with developments in online crafts marketing by subscribing to my free email *Craft Marketer Newsletter* at **www.craftmarketer.com**. See you online!

Appendix I Free and low cost resources

Build your Web site with HTML tutorials
davecentral.com
www.delorie.com/web
www.homepagenow.com/links
www.hotwired.com/webmonkey/teachingtool
www.htmlgoodies.com
www.htmlwizards.com
www.hwg.org/resources/?cid=14
www.gazoo.net/htmhell/main.html

Improve your site performance
siteinspector.linkexchange.com

Scripts for creating mail forms
www.worldwidemart.com/scripts

Shareware, freeware & free tools
www.jumbo.com
www.netfreebies.net
www.shareware.com
www.softseek.com
www.thefreesite.com
www.tucows.com
www.webmasterutilities.com
www.windows95.com
www.winsite.com

For Mac users only
hyperarchive.lcs.mit.edu/HyperArchive.html
www-personal.umich.edu/~sdamask/umich-mirrors

Free Web Pages

www.angelfire.com
www.BizLand.com
www.econgo.com
www.geocities.com
www.homestead.com
www.justwebit.com/goto.shtml
www.netfirms.com
www.virtualave.net
www.webjump.com

Web promotion

www.1x.com/promote
www.angelfire.com/hi/pelagia/links.html
www.beseen.com
www.bruceclay.com
www.foreverweb.com
www.freelinks.com
www.howtointernet.com
jimworld.com/index.html
jvmarketer.com

Reliable Web hosts for a monthly fee

www.above.net
www.communitech.net
www.serve.com
www.inetu.com
www.interland.net
www.interliant.com
www.media3.net
www.olm.net
www.rackspace.com
www.superb.net
www.tierranet.com
www.verio.com
www.webhosting.com

Free graphics, images, animations
www.clipart.co.uk
www.clipartconnection.com
www.thefreesite.com/freegraphics.htm

Free email
www.emailaddresses.com (lists over 1,000 places to get free email accounts)

Appendix II Newsletters online

Online newsletters & magazines on craft marketing

Craft Marketer News - Free. Articles and tips for selling crafts online. **www.craftmarketer.com**

Arts & Crafts Online Marketing - This an email mail list for discussing topics on online crafts marketing. Subscribe at: **www.egroups.com/group/A-C_Online_Marketing**.

The Professional Crafters Mailing List - An excellent email mail list for discussing all aspects of crafts marketing. Subscribe at: **welcome.to/professional-crafters.**

Online editions of print craft magazines

Arts Crafts Show Business - Magazine and website for the craft artisan who sells. Includes show listings, articles, links and more: **www.ArtsCraftsShowBusiness.com**

The Crafts Report - Online version of print magazine discussing all aspects of crafts business. **www.craftsreport.com**

SAC News Monthly - Articles on craft business and promotions and reviews of craft shows: **www.SACNewsmonthly.com**

Sunshine Artist - Online version of print magazine discussing art and crafts business. Also links to craft show locators. **www.sunshineartist.com**

Online resources about ecommerce

Internet Entrepreneurs Support Service. This is a discussion group for entrepreneurs and businesses doing business on the internet. Send a message with "subscribe" in the subject area to: **majordomo@ix.entreprenuers.net**

Marketing on the Internet. Send a message with "subscribe" in the subject area to: **listserv@Interent.com**

For entrepreneurs on all aspects of marketing your website. Send a message with "subscribe" in the subject area to: **listserv@citadel.net**

Online magazines about ecommerce

bizweb2000.com/sample.htm

cyberatlas.internet.com

digest.bcentral.com

jvmarketer.com

www.linkomatic.com/ezine.cgi?10000

softfornet.com/adland/list.asp

www.webbers.com/emark

www.webcommercetoday.com/wct

www.webpromote.com

www.ibm.com/thinkmag/index2.html   - IBM's Think
Leadership Magazine

www.iw.com - Internet World

Appendix III Getting Listed in Yahoo!

Yahoo! is the most important directory to be listed in. Yahoo gets many more times the traffic of any other search engine or directory. Getting listed in Yahoo should be your priority because it will mean lots more traffic for you. Go to **www.yahoo.com** and follow the links to "Suggesting Sites".

As with search engines, Yahoo ranks sites according to relevance based on keywords. The ranking is done via algorithms they keep secret. Remember that Yahoo is a directory, not a search engine. Ranking is first based on the category you submit to. Next in importance is your site title, then your site's description, and then the URL of your Web site.

Unlike the search engines, Yahoo will not spider your Web site. Each submission is handled by a live person or editor who decides if your site should be included.

Before submitting your site, make certain it is fully operable. Don't have any "under construction" pages, missing links or dead links. Yahoo editors include sites that both look good and are useful to visitors.

Your first step in getting listed is to check to see if you aren't already there. Go to **www.yahoo.com** and do a search on your URL. If your site doesn't show, decide which categories your site should be under. You get two choices for categories. How do you know what categories your site belongs under? Try searching under Yahoo for three or four of your important keywords and see what categories and subcategories come up. The submission pages ask you a series of questions about your Web site. The process is simple and step-by-step.

With Yahoo, avoid using automated submission software or service bureau (they mostly use software) submissions. It could ruin your chances for getting listed. Submit your site by hand because the categories at Yahoo change frequently making automated submissions blunder.

Yahoo has a Business Express program that allows site owners to submit their site with a promise of a review within seven days for a fee.

This service is only available to business sites. ***Caution:*** You aren't paying to get a guaranteed listing, ***only to get reviewed*** within seven days by one of their editors. They will review your site and give you a decision on whether or not they will add it.

If they decide not to list you, they tell you why and allow another free submission. It appears most sites submitted via Business Express become listed in Yahoo. Most sites submitted via the normal way do not get listed. Editors don't have time to review all the submissions.

• Make your site's title no longer than forty characters (including spaces).

• Place your keywords close to the beginning of the title.

• Use your business name as the site title.

• Ranking is alphabetical, so titles/business names beginning with "A" are shown above names with "Z". If you already have established and used a company name like "Wonder Craft," you will show up lower in Yahoo! searches.

• Construct a site description no longer than 200 characters or 25 words using your keywords toward the beginning of the description.

• Use the longest variation of your keywords. With Yahoo!, by using the word "craftwork" you will get hits when searches are entered for "craft" or "craftwork."

Appendix IV Media links

Media links

The links below will get you connected to much of the available online sites for media editors and publications:

www.bmi.net/magazines.html Online magazines
www.coalliance.org/ejournal Electronic journal database
crayon.net Free online news sources.
dir.yahoo.com/News_and_Media Yahoo media links
www.ecola.com/news Newspapers and magazines
www.elibrary.com 150 newspapers, 2,000 books, nine newswires, 800 magazines.
www.concentric.net/~stevewt 3,000 newspapers, 80 countries.
www.gebbieinc.com Database listings of media
www.imediafax.com Fax service to thousands of media desks.
www.mediafinder.com Database of print media
mfginfo.com/htm/newspapers.htm Newspapers
www.newsindex.com Newspapers
www.newsletteraccess.com Newsletters
www.newslink.org American Journalism Review contains many newspaper and magazine links
www.newspapers.com Newspapers around the world
newstation.com U.S. and international newspapers
www.niu.edu/newsplace News sources
www.online-pr.com Media links
www.owt.com/dircon Media service bureau, writes and distributes press releases
pppp.net/links/news List of news link sites
www.publist.com Directory of 150,000 publications plus 8,000 newspapers.
www.wwideweb.com/link40.htm newspaper, TV and radio news links
www.xpresspress.com - Distributes email news releases to hundreds of editors throughout the world, targeted by subject area. News release writing is also offered.

Glossary

ASCII - American Standard Code for Information Interchange - A standard protocol for pure text. Often used for sending text when you aren't sure if the other person's software can read your files.

Bandwith - Total volume of data that can move through a communications channel at a time. Usually measured in seconds.

Browser - A program that finds and displays Web pages. Examples are Netscape Navigator and Internet Explorer.

CD-Rom - Information storage medium capable of storing approximately 750 megabytes of data.

CGI - Common Gateway Interface. A transfer interface protocol for taking data from a form and sending it to a program such as an email or to a database.

Client - Mostly refers to a browser like Netscape Navigator or Internet Explorer but can also refer to a computer making contact with a host or server.

Click-through - When someone actually clicks on a banner or text link that takes them to the link's destination.

Database - Data organized in such a way as to be searched and manipulated into reports, labels, invoices, etc. An example would be a mailing list of your customers.

Domain Name - The name of a Web Site that is mapped to an IP address using a URL.

DSL (Digital Subscriber Line) - an always-on Internet connection which goes to a socket in your wall. Dozens of times faster than a modem connection. Costs vary according to provider.

Email - Messages sent via the Internet. Referred to as electronic mail.

Encryption - Coding files in such a way as to make them secure or unreadable to those without the decryption code.

FAQ - Frequently asked questions - Many large sites provide FAQ pages to answer often asked questions. The intent is that the FAQ page will take care of common problems users experience.

Flaming - Usually refers to angry responses sent via email to someone from someone else who is unhappy with the sender's SPAM.

Form - HTML code or a CGI script that is used to collect information from a visitor such as an address.

FTP - File Transfer Protocol. Protocol used to move files from one computer to another over the Internet. FTP is the method used to load your pages to your Web site.

GIF - Graphic interchange format - images on Web pages.

Home Page - The first page seen when a visitor goes to a Web site. Often called the index page or default page.

HTML - HyperText Markup Language. The code that is used to define a Web page. Don't ask me who's idea this term was.

Hyperlink - A text element, usually highlighted in blue and underlined, found on Web pages that transports the user (when clicked) to another page or Web site.

Icon - Small image or graphic representing an action or function to take. An example would be a graphic arrow that when clicked on takes the viewer to the next page.

Internet - Physical world wide interconnection between computers via TCP/IP. Connects millions of computers around the globe.

IP Address - Internet Protocol Address. The actual address where domains reside.

ISDN - Integrated services digital network - Technology available in some areas (usually large cities) that allows faster connect time to the Internet. Speeds are several times faster than 56k modems. Cost is often $30 to $40 a month.

ISP - Internet Service Provider. A company that provides Internet connection services, such as Maktrix.com/ or AOL.

JPEG - Format for graphic images found on Web pages.

Login - Usually a way of accessing a computer's files or a Web site.

Modem - A device connected to your computer that modulates data transferring it over phone lines.

Newsgroup - Discussion group online for chatting about particular subject matter.

Password - A word or series of letters and/or numbers used to access a protected file or Web site.

Server - A program or hardware device that provides a way to serve data to users.

Shareware - Software that is usually available for free trials or limited usage. Full version registration is available for a fee.

Signature - A few lines of text, usually promotional info, automatically attached at the bottom of email messages. Many email managers will create signatures for you.

SPAM - Unsolicited email sent to you to sell you something you probably don't want or need.

TCP/IP - Transmission Control Protocol/Internet Protocol. Is a communication protocol that allows computers to "talk" to each other over a physical connection like a modem.

URL - Universal Resource Locator. The address of a resource found on the World Wide Web. It usually refers to a Web page but it can also refer to any file located at the Web site.

Web page - One page located at a Web site. Usually the address of a Web page ends with .htm or .html.

Web site - A group of associated Web pages hosted at a URL address on the WWW.

Index

A

B

C

H

handling charges 124
hits 143
holidays 46
Home and Garden TV 116
HotMetal™ 27
HTML 33, 41, 86, 129, 130, 136, 149, 158

I

images 67
impressions 143
incentive programs 92
Insertion fees 119
insurance 123
Internet browsers 24
Internet commerce 13
Internet Explorer 29, 43, 105
Internet Service Provider (ISP) 21
Internet usage 14
ISDN 20

K

keyword
    9, 23, 28, 31, 40, 41, 42, 43, 65, 67, 68, 71, 72, 73, 75, 76,
79, 80, 81, 84, 86, 87, 89, 119, 122, 141, 146, 154, 155

L

Lifetime TV 116
link 82
link exchange 83, 84
links
    9, 15, 17, 34, 46, 65, 66, 67, 72, 80, 82, 83, 84, 85, 86, 87,
128, 129, 131, 134, 144, 149, 154, 156
loyalty programs 92

M

mail order 136
malls 36
marketing plan 10, 55
marketing reports 13
Martha Stewart Living 116

About the Author

James Dillehay began creating and selling his fiber art in 1984. In 1991, he published the first marketing guide ever written for fiber artisans called Weaving Profits, hailed as *"the blueprint for success in the crafts industry"* by The Crafts Report.

Author of seven books, Dillehay's craft marketing articles have reached readers of *Family Circle, The National Examiner, The Crafts Report, Better Homes & Gardens: Crafting for Profit, Sunshine Artist, Ceramics Monthly, Florida Retirement Lifestyles* and many more publications. He was a featured guest on The Carol Duvall Show, HGTV.

His book, *The Basic Guide to Selling Arts and Crafts*, was included in the training program of the Association of Creative Craft Industries (ACCI).

James is a member of the advisory board to the National Craft Association and was listed in the 1998 *Who's Who of American Entrepreneurs.*

He published the first book ever written to help craft artists understand how to successfully sell their work online in, *The Basic Guide to Selling Crafts on the Internet.*

James lives in the Manzano Mountains of New Mexico. He teaches and speaks nationally on how to achieve craft business success.

For a free email newsletter with tips and news about craft business, visit www.craftmarketer.com

Printed in the United States
15744LVS00005B/80